Performance Testing Guidance for Web Applications

patterns & practices

J.D. Meier

Carlos Farre

ıshant Bansode

Scott Barber

Dennis Rea

D1376983

Table of Contents

Chapter 2

Types of Performance Testing   17

Chapter 3

Risks Addressed Through Performance Testing   23

Part II: Exemplar Performance Testing Approaches   31

Chapter 4

Web Application Performance Testing Core Activities   33

Chapter 5

Coordinating Performance Testing with an Iteration-Based Process   49

Part III: Identify the Test Environment   103

Evaluating Systems to Increase Performance Testing Effectiveness   105

Part IV: Identify Performance Acceptance Criteria   **115**

Part VII: Analyze Results and Report   197

Part VIII: Performance Testing Techniques   235

Chapter 17

Load-Testing Web Applications   237

Chapter 18
Stress Testing Web Applications   247

Index   257

Foreword by Alberto Savoia

Foreword

Testing the performance of web applications is easy. It's easy to design unrealistic scenarios. Easy to collect and measure irrelevant performance data. And, even if you manage to design a sound scenario and collect the right data, it's easy to use the wrong statistical methods to summarize and present the results.

Starting in the late '90s, through the peak of the Internet bubble and beyond, I spent a lot of time testing the performance of web applications. During that period, I designed and led several mission-critical web performance and load tests for high-profile Internet companies. Working with the in-house performance *experts* at each company was very revealing — and quite frightening. Most of the engineers assigned to work on web application performance were smart, hard-working, and dedicated; they invested in expensive software and hardware, read the right books, and followed the *best practices* of the day. But, somehow, the results of their performance measurements and predictions did not match reality. In some cases the performance tests *over*estimated the performance and scalability of the web applications — leading to embarrassing and costly crashes when the web application was deployed. In other cases, they *under*estimated capacity and scalability — leading to unnecessary spending on hardware and infrastructure. The errors in these tests were not small; some tests overestimated or underestimated actual performance and capacity by an order of magnitude or more! How is this possible?

Based on my experience, the majority of gross errors in web application performance testing are the result of oversimplification. More precisely, they are the result oversimplification of user behavior and oversimplification in summarizing and reporting test results. Imagine a transportation engineer estimating traffic patterns for a proposed stretch of highway by assuming that most drivers will drive at the same average speed, break and accelerate with the same response time and at the same rate, and never change lanes. A simple — but completely worthless — scenario. Or imagine the same transportation engineer reporting that there are no traffic issues because the average speed is 57mph — without bringing up that during rush-hour the average speed is 25mph. A simple, but very misleading, result. Unfortunately, most web application performance testers commit errors of oversimplification as bad, or worse, as the ones committed by our hypothetical transportation engineer.

I am all for simplicity but, as Albert Einstein once said: "Make everything as simple as possible, but not simpler." When it comes to testing the performance of web applications, that's exactly what this remarkable — and much needed — book teaches you. The authors leverage their passion, experience, and hard-earned knowledge and provide you with the broad, thorough, and extensible foundation you need to tackle web performance testing the right way. *Performance Testing Guidance for Web Applications* does not get bogged down with unnecessary details, but it does make sure that you know about — and don't overlook — the key parameters and variables that you need to take into account in designing, conducting, and analyzing your tests.

If you are new to web performance testing, this book will get you started on the right path and save you a lot of time and embarrassment. Even if you are a seasoned web performance testing veteran, I am confident that this book will provide you with new insights and, most likely, have you slap your forehead a few times as you read about some common and familiar mistakes. In either case, *Performance Testing Guidance for Web Applications*, is a must-have for any web performance engineer bookshelf.

Alberto Savoia

Founder and CTO, Agitar Software Inc.

July, 2007

Author of: *"The Science and Art of Web Site Load Testing"*, *"Web Load Test Planning"*, and *"Trade Secrets from a Web Testing Expert"*.

Foreword by Rico Mariani

Foreword

It's hard to imagine anything than is considered a more arcane art than performance tuning—unless perhaps it is performance testing.

If you were to go door to door between groups just within Microsoft you would find many different approaches with various different degrees of quality or success. Pretty much everyone will vow that their approach is certainly the one that is best for them—except maybe an honest few, who might say something more modest. Some have good reason to be confident because they really have studied the space very well. In my own experience at least, the situation is not altogether different outside of Microsoft than it is inside where I do my work. It's a mixed bag, on a good day.

If I had to describe the most common problem I see in this space with one word it would imbalance. There are many aspects to testing and teams tend to unduly focus on one or another and then sometimes get blindsided by the ones they missed. Perhaps they're only thinking about throughput—what about consumption? Perhaps only latency—what about smooth delivery? Perhaps only cost—what about scalability?

You get great performance by balancing the key factors, considering them in your designs and then tracking them carefully. So perhaps the greatest service that a book like Performance Testing Guidance for Web Applications can provide to you is a broader understanding of what all the factors might be so that you have an excellent menu of considerations to choose from in your testing plan. Luckily, that is just what you're going to get.

The Guidance that follows provides a great survey of the most important considerations: From how to understand and quantify your desired end user experience, how to choose key resources for study, to advice on summarizing results in a statistically meaningful way, and how to fit these practices into different software lifecycles. And even though the focus is squarely on web applications, the teachings are actually much more general and can easily be applied for many different kinds of applications.

Great engineering comes from creating predictable results at predictable costs. In fact, I like to say that if you're not measuring you're not engineering. This volume will provide you with the performance testing fundamentals to give you the ongoing metrics you need to do great engineering.

Rico Mariani

Chief Architect of Visual Studio

Microsoft Corporation

July, 2007

Rico Mariani began his career at Microsoft in 1988, working on language products beginning with Microsoft® C version 6.0, and contributed there until the release of the Microsoft Visual C++® version 5.0 development system. In 1995, Rico became development manager for what was to become the "Sidewalk" project, which started his 7 years of platform work on various MSN technologies. In the summer of 2002, Rico returned to the Developer Division to as a Performance Architect on the CLR team. His performance work led to his most recent assignment as Chief Architect of Visual Studio. Rico's interests include compilers and language theory, databases, 3-D art, and good fiction.

Introduction

Performance Testing Guidance for Web Applications provides an end-to-end approach for implementing performance testing. Whether you are new to performance testing or looking for ways to improve your current performance-testing approach, you will gain insights that you can tailor to your specific scenarios.

The information in this guide is based on applied use in customer scenarios. It reflects the lessons learned from multiple performance-testing professionals. The guidance is task-based and presented in the following parts:

- **Part 1, "Introduction to Performance Testing,"** gives you an overview of common types of performance testing, key concepts, and a set of common terms used in performance testing.
- **Part II, "Exemplar Performance Testing Approaches,"** shows you seven core activities for performance testing. This section also contains information designed to show you how to apply performance testing to different environments, including Agile and CMMI® software development.
- **Part III, "Identify the Test Environment,"** shows you how to collect information about your project that you will need for your performance tests. This includes collecting information on system architecture, the physical deployment, user activities, and any relevant batch processes.
- **Part IV, "Identify Performance Acceptance Criteria,"** shows you how to determine your performance testing objectives. You will also learn how to achieve clarity around your various performance goals and requirements, from a performance testing perspective.
- **Part V, "Plan and Design Tests,"** shows you how to model the workload and user experience to design more effective performance tests.
- **Part VI, "Execute Tests,"** walks you through the main activities of actual performance testing.
- **Part VII, "Analyze Results and Report,"** shows you how to organize and present your findings in a way that is useful based on the audience and the intent of the report.
- **Part VIII, "Performance-Testing Techniques,"** shows you the core techniques for performing load and stress testing.

Scope of This Guide

This guide is focused on Web application performance testing. It provides recommendations on the following:

- Managing and conducting performance testing in both dynamic (e.g., Agile) and structured (e.g., CMMI) environments.
- Performance testing, including load testing, stress testing, and other types of performance related testing.
- Core activities of performance testing: identifying objectives, designing tests, executing tests, analyzing results, and reporting.

Even though many of the topics addressed in this guide apply equally well to other types of applications, the topics are all explained from a Web application perspective for consistency and to ensure that the concepts are presented in a manner that is most intuitive to the majority of anticipated readers.

This guide is intended to be tool-agnostic. What that means is that none of the concepts presented in this guide require any specific tool to accomplish, though some techniques or concepts will require the use of a certain class of tools.

This guide does not directly address performance tuning. Performance tuning is extremely application- and technology-specific and thus is not a good fit for the style and format of the guide. The guide does, however, address high-level approaches around how performance testing and performance tuning activities overlap and feed one another.

Why We Wrote This Guide

We wrote this guide to accomplish the following:

- To consolidate real-world lessons learned around performance testing.
- To present a roadmap for end-to-end performance testing.
- To narrow the gap between state of the art and state of the practice.

Features of This Guide

- **Approach for performance testing.** The guide provides an approach that organizes performance testing into logical units to help you incrementally adopt performance testing throughout your application life cycle.
- **Principles and practices.** These serve as the foundation for the guide and provide a stable basis for recommendations. They also reflect successful approaches used in the field.

- **Processes and methodologies.** These provide steps for managing and conducting performance testing. For simplification and tangible results, they are broken down into activities with inputs, outputs, and steps. You can use the steps as a baseline or to help you evolve your own process.

- **Life cycle approach.** The guide provides end-to-end guidance on managing performance testing throughout your application life cycle, to reduce risk and lower total cost of ownership (TCO).

- **Modular.** Each chapter within the guide is designed to be read independently. You do not need to read the guide from beginning to end to benefit from it. Use the parts you need.

- **Holistic.** The guide is designed with the end in mind. If you do read the guide from beginning to end, it is organized to fit together in a comprehensive way. The guide, in its entirety, is better than the sum of its parts.

- **Subject matter expertise.** The guide exposes insight from various experts throughout Microsoft and from customers in the field.

Who Should Read This Guide

This guide is targeted at providing individuals with the resources, patterns, and practices they need to conduct effective performance testing.

How to Use This Guide

You can read this guide from beginning to end, or you can read only the relevant parts or chapters. You can adopt the guide in its entirety for your organization or you can use critical components to address your highest-priority needs.

Ways to Use the Guide

There are many ways to use this comprehensive guidance. The following are some suggestions:

- **Use it as a mentor.** Use the guide as your mentor for learning how to conduct performance testing. The guide encapsulates the lessons learned and experiences gained by many subject matter experts.

- **Use it as a reference.** Use the guide as a reference for learning the do's and don'ts of performance testing.

- **Incorporate performance testing into your application development life cycle.** Adopt the approach and practices that work for you and incorporate them into your application life cycle.

- **Use it when you design your performance tests.** Design applications using the principles and best practices presented in this guide. Benefit from lessons learned.
- **Create training.** Create training based on the concepts and techniques used throughout the guide.

Organization of This Guide

You can read this guide from end to end, or you can read only the chapters you need to do your job.

Parts

The guide is divided into eight parts:

- Part 1, Introduction to Performance Testing
- Part II, Exemplar Performance Testing Approaches
- Part III, Identify the Test Environment
- Part IV, Identify Performance Acceptance Criteria
- Part V, Plan and Design Tests
- Part VI, Execute Tests
- Part VII, Analyze Results and Report
- Part VIII, Performance-Testing Techniques

Part 1, Introduction to Performance Testing

- Chapter 1, "Fundamentals of Web Application Performance Testing"
- Chapter 2, "Types of Performance Testing"
- Chapter 3, "Risks Addressed Through Performance Testing"

Part II, Exemplar Performance Testing Approaches

- Chapter 4, "Web Application Performance Testing Core Activities"
- Chapter 5, "Coordinating Performance Testing with an Iteration-Based Process"
- Chapter 6, "Managing an Agile Performance Test Cycle"
- Chapter 7, "Managing the Performance Test Cycle in a Regulated (CMMI) Environment"

Part III, Identify the Test Environment

- Chapter 8, "Evaluating Systems to Increase Performance-Testing Effectiveness"

Part IV, Identify Performance Acceptance Criteria

- Chapter 9, "Determining Performance Testing Objectives"
- Chapter 10, "Quantifying End-User Response Time Goals"
- Chapter 11, "Consolidating Various Types of Performance Acceptance Criteria"

Part V, Plan and Design Tests

- Chapter 12, "Modeling Application Usage"
- Chapter 13, "Determining Individual User Data and Variances"

Part VI, Execute Tests

- Chapter 14, "Test Execution"

Part VII, Analyze Results and Report

- Chapter 15, "Key Mathematic Principles for Performance Testers"
- Chapter 16, "Performance Test Reporting Fundamentals"

Part VIII, Performance-Testing Techniques

- Chapter 17, "Load-Testing Web Applications"
- Chapter 18, "Stress-Testing Web Applications"

Approach Used in This Guide

The primary task of any testing activity is to collect information in order to be able to help stakeholders make informed decisions related to the overall quality of the application being tested. Performance testing additionally tends to focus on helping to identify bottlenecks in a system, tuning a system, establishing a baseline for future testing, and determining compliance with performance goals and requirements. In addition, the results from performance testing and analysis can help you to estimate the hardware configuration required to support the application(s) when you "go live" to production operation.

```
┌─────────────────────────────────────────┐
│ │ Core Performance Testing Activities │ │
│ ┌─────────────────────────────────────┐ │
│ │ 1. Identify Test Environment        │ │
│ └─────────────────────────────────────┘ │
│ ┌─────────────────────────────────────┐ │
│ │ 2. Identify Performance Acceptance Criteria │
│ └─────────────────────────────────────┘ │
│ ┌─────────────────────────────────────┐ │
│ │ 3. Plan and Design Tests            │ │
│ └─────────────────────────────────────┘ │
│ ┌─────────────────────────────────────┐ │
│ │ 4. Configure Test Environment       │ │
│ └─────────────────────────────────────┘ │
│ ┌─────────────────────────────────────┐ │
│ │ 5. Implement Test Design            │ │
│ └─────────────────────────────────────┘ │
│ ┌─────────────────────────────────────┐ │
│ │ 6. Execute Tests                    │ │
│ └─────────────────────────────────────┘ │
│ ┌─────────────────────────────────────┐ │
│ │ 7. Analyze, Report, and Retest      │ │
│ └─────────────────────────────────────┘ │
└─────────────────────────────────────────┘
```

The performance-testing approach used in this guide consists of the following activities:

- **Activity 1. Identify the Test Environment.** Identify the physical test environment and the production environment as well as the tools and resources available to the test team. The physical environment includes hardware, software, and network configurations. Having a thorough understanding of the entire test environment at the outset enables more efficient test design and planning and helps you identify testing challenges early in the project. In some situations, this process must be revisited periodically throughout the project's life cycle.

- **Activity 2. Identify Performance Acceptance Criteria.** Identify the response time, throughput, and resource utilization goals and constraints. In general, response time is a user concern, throughput is a business concern, and resource utilization is a system concern. Additionally, identify project success criteria that may not be captured by those goals and constraints; for example, using performance tests to evaluate what combination of configuration settings will result in the most desirable performance characteristics.

- **Activity 3. Plan and Design Tests.** Identify key scenarios, determine variability among representative users and how to simulate that variability, define test data, and establish metrics to be collected. Consolidate this information into one or more models of system usage to be implemented, executed, and analyzed.

- **Activity 4. Configure the Test Environment.** Prepare the test environment, tools, and resources necessary to execute each strategy as features and components become available for test. Ensure that the test environment is instrumented for resource monitoring as necessary.

- **Activity 5. Implement the Test Design.** Develop the performance tests in accordance with the test design.

- **Activity 6. Execute the Test.** Run and monitor your tests. Validate the tests, test data, and results collection. Execute validated tests for analysis while monitoring the test and the test environment.

- **Activity 7. Analyze Results, Report, and Retest.** Consolidate and share results data. Analyze the data both individually and as a cross-functional team. Reprioritize the remaining tests and re-execute them as needed. When all of the metric values are within accepted limits, none of the set thresholds have been violated, and all of the desired information has been collected, you have finished testing that particular scenario on that particular configuration.

Feedback on the Guide

We have made every effort to ensure the accuracy of this guide and its companion content. If you have comments on this guide, send e-mail to:

PerfTest@microsoft.com

We are particularly interested in feedback regarding the following:

- Technical issues specific to recommendations
- Usefulness and usability issues

The Team Who Brought You This Guide

This guide was created by the following team members:

- J.D. Meier
- Carlos Farre
- Prashant Bansode
- Scott Barber
- Dennis Rea

Contributors and Reviewers

Alan Ridlehoover; Clint Huffman; Edmund Wong; Ken Perilman; Larry Brader; Mark Tomlinson; Paul Williams; Pete Coupland; Rico Mariani

External Contributors and Reviewers

Alberto Savoia; Ben Simo; Cem Kaner; Chris Loosley; Corey Goldberg; Dawn Haynes; Derek Mead; Karen N. Johnson; Mike Bonar; Pradeep Soundararajan; Richard Leeke; Roland Stens; Ross Collard; Steven Woody

Tell Us About Your Success

If this guide helps you, we would like to know. Please tell us by writing a short summary of the problems you faced and how this guide helped you out. Submit your summary to:

MyStory@Microsoft.com

Part I
Introduction to Performance Testing

In this part:
- Fundamentals of Web Application Performance Testing
- Types of Performance Testing
- Risks Addressed Through Performance Testing

1

Fundamentals of Web Application Performance Testing

Objectives

- Learn what performance testing is.
- Learn the core activities of performance testing.
- Learn why performance testing matters.
- Learn about the relevance of project context to performance testing.
- Learn how tuning fits into the performance testing cycle.

Overview

Performance testing is a type of testing intended to determine the responsiveness, throughput, reliability, and/or scalability of a system under a given workload. Performance testing is commonly conducted to accomplish the following:

- Assess production readiness
- Evaluate against performance criteria
- Compare performance characteristics of multiple systems or system configurations
- Find the source of performance problems
- Support system tuning
- Find throughput levels

This chapter provides a set of foundational building blocks on which to base your understanding of performance testing principles, ultimately leading to successful performance-testing projects. Additionally, this chapter introduces various terms and concepts used throughout this guide.

How to Use This Chapter

Use this chapter to understand the purpose of performance testing and the core activities that it entails. To get the most from this chapter:

- Use the "Project Context" section to understand how to focus on the relevant items during performance testing.
- Use the "Relationship Between Performance Testing and Tuning" section to understand the relationship between performance testing and performance tuning, and to understand the overall performance tuning process.
- Use the "Performance, Load, and Stress Testing" section to understand various types of performance testing.
- Use the "Baselines" and "Benchmarking" sections to understand the various methods of performance comparison that you can use to evaluate your application.
- Use the "Terminology" section to understand the common terminology for performance testing that will facilitate articulating terms correctly in the context of your project.

Core Activities of Performance Testing

Performance testing is typically done to help identify bottlenecks in a system, establish a baseline for future testing, support a performance tuning effort, determine compliance with performance goals and requirements, and/or collect other performance-related data to help stakeholders make informed decisions related to the overall quality of the application being tested. In addition, the results from performance testing and analysis can help you to estimate the hardware configuration required to support the application(s) when you "go live" to production operation.

Figure 1.1 *Core Performance Testing Activities*

The performance testing approach used in this guide consists of the following activities:

1. **Activity 1. Identify the Test Environment.** Identify the physical test environment and the production environment as well as the tools and resources available to the test team. The physical environment includes hardware, software, and network configurations. Having a thorough understanding of the entire test environment at the outset enables more efficient test design and planning and helps you identify testing challenges early in the project. In some situations, this process must be revisited periodically throughout the project's life cycle.

2. **Activity 2. Identify Performance Acceptance Criteria.** Identify the response time, throughput, and resource utilization goals and constraints. In general, response time is a user concern, throughput is a business concern, and resource utilization is a system concern. Additionally, identify project success criteria that may not be captured by those goals and constraints; for example, using performance tests to evaluate what combination of configuration settings will result in the most desirable performance characteristics.

3. **Activity 3. Plan and Design Tests.** Identify key scenarios, determine variability among representative users and how to simulate that variability, define test data, and establish metrics to be collected. Consolidate this information into one or more models of system usage to be implemented, executed, and analyzed.

4. **Activity 4. Configure the Test Environment.** Prepare the test environment, tools, and resources necessary to execute each strategy as features and components become available for test. Ensure that the test environment is instrumented for resource monitoring as necessary.

5. **Activity 5. Implement the Test Design.** Develop the performance tests in accordance with the test design.

6. **Activity 6. Execute the Test.** Run and monitor your tests. Validate the tests, test data, and results collection. Execute validated tests for analysis while monitoring the test and the test environment.

7. **Activity 7. Analyze Results, Report, and Retest.** Consolidate and share results data. Analyze the data both individually and as a cross-functional team. Reprioritize the remaining tests and re-execute them as needed. When all of the metric values are within accepted limits, none of the set thresholds have been violated, and all of the desired information has been collected, you have finished testing that particular scenario on that particular configuration.

Why Do Performance Testing?

At the highest level, performance testing is almost always conducted to address one or more risks related to expense, opportunity costs, continuity, and/or corporate reputation. Some more specific reasons for conducting performance testing include:

- Assessing release readiness by:
  - Enabling you to predict or estimate the performance characteristics of an application in production and evaluate whether or not to address performance concerns based on those predictions. These predictions are also valuable to the stakeholders who make decisions about whether an application is ready for release or capable of handling future growth, or whether it requires a performance improvement/hardware upgrade prior to release.
  - Providing data indicating the likelihood of user dissatisfaction with the performance characteristics of the system.
  - Providing data to aid in the prediction of revenue losses or damaged brand credibility due to scalability or stability issues, or due to users being dissatisfied with application response time.
- Assessing infrastructure adequacy by:
  - Evaluating the adequacy of current capacity.
  - Determining the acceptability of stability.
  - Determining the capacity of the application's infrastructure, as well as determining the future resources required to deliver acceptable application performance.
  - Comparing different system configurations to determine which works best for both the application and the business.
  - Verifying that the application exhibits the desired performance characteristics, within budgeted resource utilization constraints.

- Assessing adequacy of developed software performance by:
  - Determining the application's desired performance characteristics before and after changes to the software.
  - Providing comparisons between the application's current and desired performance characteristics.
- Improving the efficiency of performance tuning by:
  - Analyzing the behavior of the application at various load levels.
  - Identifying bottlenecks in the application.
  - Providing information related to the speed, scalability, and stability of a product prior to production release, thus enabling you to make informed decisions about whether and when to tune the system.

Project Context

For a performance testing project to be successful, both the approach to testing performance and the testing itself must be relevant to the context of the project. Without an understanding of the project context, performance testing is bound to focus on only those items that the performance tester or test team assumes to be important, as opposed to those that truly are important, frequently leading to wasted time, frustration, and conflicts.

The project context is nothing more than those things that are, or may become, relevant to achieving project success. This may include, but is not limited to:

- The overall vision or intent of the project
- Performance testing objectives
- Performance success criteria
- The development life cycle
- The project schedule
- The project budget
- Available tools and environments
- The skill set of the performance tester and the team
- The priority of detected performance concerns
- The business impact of deploying an application that performs poorly

Some examples of items that may be relevant to the performance-testing effort in your project context include:

- **Project vision.** Before beginning performance testing, ensure that you understand the current project vision. The project vision is the foundation for determining what performance testing is necessary and valuable. Revisit the vision regularly, as it has the potential to change as well.

- **Purpose of the system.** Understand the purpose of the application or system you are testing. This will help you identify the highest-priority performance characteristics on which you should focus your testing. You will need to know the system's intent, the actual hardware and software architecture deployed, and the characteristics of the typical end user.

- **Customer or user expectations.** Keep customer or user expectations in mind when planning performance testing. Remember that customer or user satisfaction is based on expectations, not simply compliance with explicitly stated requirements.

- **Business drivers.** Understand the business drivers – such as business needs or opportunities – that are constrained to some degree by budget, schedule, and/or resources. It is important to meet your business requirements on time and within the available budget.

- **Reasons for testing performance.** Understand the reasons for conducting performance testing very early in the project. Failing to do so might lead to ineffective performance testing. These reasons often go beyond a list of performance acceptance criteria and are bound to change or shift priority as the project progresses, so revisit them regularly as you and your team learn more about the application, its performance, and the customer or user.

- **Value that performance testing brings to the project.** Understand the value that performance testing is expected to bring to the project by translating the project- and business-level objectives into specific, identifiable, and manageable performance testing activities. Coordinate and prioritize these activities to determine which performance testing activities are likely to add value.

- **Project management and staffing.** Understand the team's organization, operation, and communication techniques in order to conduct performance testing effectively.

- **Process.** Understand your team's process and interpret how that process applies to performance testing. If the team's process documentation does not address performance testing directly, extrapolate the document to include performance testing to the best of your ability, and then get the revised document approved by the project manager and/or process engineer.

- **Compliance criteria.** Understand the regulatory requirements related to your project. Obtain compliance documents to ensure that you have the specific language and context of any statement related to testing, as this information is critical to determining compliance tests and ensuring a compliant product. Also understand that the nature of performance testing makes it virtually impossible to follow the same processes that have been developed for functional testing.

- **Project schedule.** Be aware of the project start and end dates, the hardware and environment availability dates, the flow of builds and releases, and any checkpoints and milestones in the project schedule.

The Relationship Between Performance Testing and Tuning

When end-to-end performance testing reveals system or application characteristics that are deemed unacceptable, many teams shift their focus from performance testing to performance tuning, to discover what is necessary to make the application perform acceptably. A team may also shift its focus to tuning when performance criteria have been met but the team wants to reduce the amount of resources being used in order to increase platform headroom, decrease the volume of hardware needed, and/or further improve system performance.

Cooperative Effort

Although tuning is not the direct responsibility of most performance testers, the tuning process is most effective when it is a cooperative effort between all of those concerned with the application or system under test, including:

- Product vendors
- Architects
- Developers
- Testers
- Database administrators
- System administrators
- Network administrators

Without the cooperation of a cross-functional team, it is almost impossible to gain the system-wide perspective necessary to resolve performance issues effectively or efficiently.

The performance tester, or performance testing team, is a critical component of this cooperative team as tuning typically requires additional monitoring of components, resources, and response times under a variety of load conditions and configurations. Generally speaking, it is the performance tester who has the tools and expertise to provide this information in an efficient manner, making the performance tester the enabler for tuning.

Tuning Process Overview

Tuning follows an iterative process that is usually separate from, but not independent of, the performance testing approach a project is following. The following is a brief overview of a typical tuning process:

- Tests are conducted with the system or application deployed in a well-defined, controlled test environment in order to ensure that the configuration and test results at the start of the testing process are known and reproducible.

- When the tests reveal performance characteristics deemed to be unacceptable, the performance testing and tuning team enters a diagnosis and remediation stage (tuning) that will require changes to be applied to the test environment and/or the application. It is not uncommon to make temporary changes that are deliberately designed to magnify an issue for diagnostic purposes, or to change the test environment to see if such changes lead to better performance.

- The cooperative testing and tuning team is generally given full and exclusive control over the test environment in order to maximize the effectiveness of the tuning phase.

- Performance tests are executed, or re-executed after each change to the test environment, in order to measure the impact of a remedial change.

- The tuning process typically involves a rapid sequence of changes and tests. This process can take exponentially more time if a cooperative testing and tuning team is not fully available and dedicated to this effort while in a tuning phase.

- When a tuning phase is complete, the test environment is generally reset to its initial state, the successful remedial changes are applied again, and any unsuccessful remedial changes (together with temporary instrumentation and diagnostic changes) are discarded. The performance test should then be repeated to prove that the correct changes have been identified. It might also be the case that the test environment itself is changed to reflect new expectations as to the minimal required production environment. This is unusual, but a potential outcome of the tuning effort.

Performance, Load, and Stress Testing

Performance tests are usually described as belonging to one of the following three categories:

- **Performance testing.** This type of testing determines or validates the speed, scalability, and/or stability characteristics of the system or application under test. Performance is concerned with achieving response times, throughput, and resource-utilization levels that meet the performance objectives for the project or product. In this guide, performance testing represents the superset of all of the other subcategories of performance-related testing.

- **Load testing.** This subcategory of performance testing is focused on determining or validating performance characteristics of the system or application under test when subjected to workloads and load volumes anticipated during production operations.

- **Stress testing.** This subcategory of performance testing is focused on determining or validating performance characteristics of the system or application under test when subjected to conditions beyond those anticipated during production operations. Stress tests may also include tests focused on determining or validating performance characteristics of the system or application under test when subjected to other stressful conditions, such as limited memory, insufficient disk space, or server failure. These tests are designed to determine under what conditions an application will fail, how it will fail, and what indicators can be monitored to warn of an impending failure.

Baselines

Creating a baseline is the process of running a set of tests to capture performance metric data for the purpose of evaluating the effectiveness of subsequent performance-improving changes to the system or application. A critical aspect of a baseline is that all characteristics and configuration options except those specifically being varied for comparison must remain invariant. Once a part of the system that is not intentionally being varied for comparison to the baseline is changed, the baseline measurement is no longer a valid basis for comparison.

With respect to Web applications, you can use a baseline to determine whether performance is improving or declining and to find deviations across different builds and versions. For example, you could measure load time, the number of transactions processed per unit of time, the number of Web pages served per unit of time, and resource utilization such as memory usage and processor usage. Some considerations about using baselines include:

- **A baseline can be created for a system, component, or application.** A baseline can also be created for different layers of the application, including a database, Web services, and so on.

- **A baseline can set the standard for comparison, to track future optimizations or regressions.** It is important to validate that the baseline results are repeatable, because considerable fluctuations may occur across test results due to environment and workload characteristics.

- **Baselines can help identify changes in performance.** Baselines can help product teams identify changes in performance that reflect degradation or optimization over the course of the development life cycle. Identifying these changes in comparison to a well-known state or configuration often makes resolving performance issues simpler.

- **Baselines assets should be reusable.** Baselines are most valuable if they are created by using a set of reusable test assets. It is important that such tests accurately simulate repeatable and actionable workload characteristics.

- **Baselines are metrics.** Baseline results can be articulated by using a broad set of key performance indicators, including response time, processor capacity, memory usage, disk capacity, and network bandwidth.

- **Baselines act as a shared frame of reference.** Sharing baseline results allows your team to build a common store of acquired knowledge about the performance characteristics of an application or component.

- **Avoid over-generalizing your baselines.** If your project entails a major reengineering of the application, you need to reestablish the baseline for testing that application. A baseline is application-specific and is most useful for comparing performance across different versions. Sometimes, subsequent versions of an application are so different that previous baselines are no longer valid for comparisons.

- **Know your application's behavior.** It is a good idea to ensure that you completely understand the behavior of the application at the time a baseline is created. Failure to do so before making changes to the system with a focus on optimization objectives is frequently counterproductive.

- **Baselines evolve.** At times you will have to redefine your baseline because of changes that have been made to the system since the time the baseline was initially captured.

Benchmarking

Benchmarking is the process of comparing your system's performance against a baseline that you have created internally or against an industry standard endorsed by some other organization.

In the case of a Web application, you would run a set of tests that comply with the specifications of an industry benchmark in order to capture the performance metrics necessary to determine your application's benchmark score. You can then compare your application against other systems or applications that also calculated their score for the same benchmark. You may choose to tune your application performance to achieve or surpass a certain benchmark score. Some considerations about benchmarking include:

- **You need to play by the rules.** A benchmark is achieved by working with industry specifications or by porting an existing implementation to meet such standards. Benchmarking entails identifying all of the necessary components that will run together, the market where the product exists, and the specific metrics to be measured.

- **Because you play by the rules, you can be transparent.** Benchmarking results can be published to the outside world. Since comparisons may be produced by your competitors, you will want to employ a strict set of standard approaches for testing and data to ensure reliable results.

- **You divulge results across various metrics.** Performance metrics may involve load time, number of transactions processed per unit of time, Web pages accessed per unit of time, processor usage, memory usage, search times, and so on.

Terminology

The following definitions are used throughout this guide. Every effort has been made to ensure that these terms and definitions are consistent with formal use and industry standards; however, some of these terms are known to have certain valid alternate definitions and implications in specific industries and organizations. Keep in mind that these definitions are intended to aid communication and are not an attempt to create a universal standard.

Term / Concept	Description
Capacity	The *capacity* of a system is the total workload it can handle without violating predetermined key performance acceptance criteria.
Capacity test	A *capacity test* complements load testing by determining your server's ultimate failure point, whereas load testing monitors results at various levels of load and traffic patterns. You perform capacity testing in conjunction with capacity planning, which you use to plan for future growth, such as an increased user base or increased volume of data. For example, to accommodate future loads, you need to know how many additional resources (such as processor capacity, memory usage, disk capacity, or network bandwidth) are necessary to support future usage levels. Capacity testing helps you to identify a scaling strategy in order to determine whether you should scale up or scale out.
Component test	A *component test* is any performance test that targets an architectural component of the application. Commonly tested components include servers, databases, networks, firewalls, and storage devices.
Endurance test	An *endurance test* is a type of performance test focused on determining or validating performance characteristics of the product under test when subjected to workload models and load volumes anticipated during production operations over an extended period of time. Endurance testing is a subset of load testing.
Investigation	*Investigation* is an activity based on collecting information related to the speed, scalability, and/or stability characteristics of the product under test that may have value in determining or improving product quality. Investigation is frequently employed to prove or disprove hypotheses regarding the root cause of one or more observed performance issues.
Latency	*Latency* is a measure of responsiveness that represents the time it takes to complete the execution of a request. Latency may also represent the sum of several latencies or subtasks.

continued

Term / Concept	Description
Metrics	*Metrics* are measurements obtained by running performance tests as expressed on a commonly understood scale. Some metrics commonly obtained through performance tests include processor utilization over time and memory usage by load.
Performance	*Performance* refers to information regarding your application's response times, throughput, and resource utilization levels.
Performance test	A *performance test* is a technical investigation done to determine or validate the speed, scalability, and/or stability characteristics of the product under test. Performance testing is the superset containing all other subcategories of performance testing described in this chapter.
Performance budgets or allocations	*Performance budgets* (or *allocations*) are constraints placed on developers regarding allowable resource consumption for their component.
Performance goals	*Performance goals* are the criteria that your team wants to meet before product release, although these criteria may be negotiable under certain circumstances. For example, if a response time goal of three seconds is set for a particular transaction but the actual response time is 3.3 seconds, it is likely that the stakeholders will choose to release the application and defer performance tuning of that transaction for a future release.
Performance objectives	*Performance objectives* are usually specified in terms of response times, throughput (transactions per second), and resource-utilization levels and typically focus on metrics that can be directly related to user satisfaction.
Performance requirements	*Performance requirements* are those criteria that are absolutely non-negotiable due to contractual obligations, service level agreements (SLAs), or fixed business needs. Any performance criterion that will not unquestionably lead to a decision to delay a release until the criterion passes is not absolutely required and therefore, not a requirement.
Performance targets	*Performance targets* are the desired values for the metrics identified for your project under a particular set of conditions, usually specified in terms of response time, throughput, and resource-utilization levels. Resource-utilization levels include the amount of processor capacity, memory, disk I/O, and network I/O that your application consumes. Performance targets typically equate to project goals.
Performance testing objectives	*Performance testing objectives* refer to data collected through the performance-testing process that is anticipated to have value in determining or improving product quality. However, these objectives are not necessarily quantitative or directly related to a performance requirement, goal, or stated quality of service (QoS) specification.
Performance thresholds	*Performance thresholds* are the maximum acceptable values for the metrics identified for your project, usually specified in terms of response time, throughput (transactions per second), and resource-utilization levels. Resource-utilization levels include the amount of processor capacity, memory, disk I/O, and network I/O that your application consumes. Performance thresholds typically equate to requirements.

Term / Concept	Description
Resource utilization	*Resource utilization* is the cost of the project in terms of system resources. The primary resources are processor, memory, disk I/O, and network I/O.
Response time	*Response time* is a measure of how responsive an application or subsystem is to a client request.
Saturation	*Saturation* refers to the point at which a resource has reached full utilization.
Scalability	*Scalability* refers to an application's ability to handle additional workload, without adversely affecting performance, by adding resources such as processor, memory, and storage capacity.
Scenarios	In the context of performance testing, a *scenario* is a sequence of steps in your application. A scenario can represent a use case or a business function such as searching a product catalog, adding an item to a shopping cart, or placing an order.
Smoke test	A *smoke test* is the initial run of a performance test to see if your application can perform its operations under a normal load.
Spike test	A *spike test* is a type of performance test focused on determining or validating performance characteristics of the product under test when subjected to workload models and load volumes that repeatedly increase beyond anticipated production operations for short periods of time. Spike testing is a subset of stress testing.
Stability	In the context of performance testing, *stability* refers to the overall reliability, robustness, functional and data integrity, availability, and/or consistency of responsiveness for your system under a variety conditions.
Stress test	A *stress test* is a type of performance test designed to evaluate an application's behavior when it is pushed beyond normal or peak load conditions. The goal of stress testing is to reveal application bugs that surface only under high load conditions. These bugs can include such things as synchronization issues, race conditions, and memory leaks. Stress testing enables you to identify your application's weak points, and shows how the application behaves under extreme load conditions.
Throughput	*Throughput* is the number of units of work that can be handled per unit of time; for instance, requests per second, calls per day, hits per second, reports per year, etc.
Unit test	In the context of performance testing, a *unit test* is any test that targets a module of code where that module is any logical subset of the entire existing code base of the application, with a focus on performance characteristics. Commonly tested modules include functions, procedures, routines, objects, methods, and classes. Performance unit tests are frequently created and conducted by the developer who wrote the module of code being tested.
Utilization	In the context of performance testing, *utilization* is the percentage of time that a resource is busy servicing user requests. The remaining percentage of time is considered idle time.

continued

Term / Concept	Description
Validation test	A *validation test* compares the speed, scalability, and/or stability characteristics of the product under test against the expectations that have been set or presumed for that product.
Workload	*Workload* is the stimulus applied to a system, application, or component to simulate a usage pattern, in regard to concurrency and/or data inputs. The workload includes the total number of users, concurrent active users, data volumes, and transaction volumes, along with the transaction mix. For performance modeling, you associate a workload with an individual scenario.

Summary

Performance testing helps to identify bottlenecks in a system, establish a baseline for future testing, support a performance tuning effort, and determine compliance with performance goals and requirements. Including performance testing very early in your development life cycle tends to add significant value to the project.

For a performance testing project to be successful, the testing must be relevant to the context of the project, which helps you to focus on the items that that are truly important.

If the performance characteristics are unacceptable, you will typically want to shift the focus from performance testing to performance tuning in order to make the application perform acceptably. You will likely also focus on tuning if you want to reduce the amount of resources being used and/or further improve system performance.

Performance, load, and stress tests are subcategories of performance testing, each intended for a different purpose.

Creating a baseline against which to evaluate the effectiveness of subsequent performance-improving changes to the system or application will generally increase project efficiency.

2

Types of Performance Testing

Objectives

- Learn about various types of performance tests.
- Understand the values and benefits associated with each type of performance testing.
- Understand the potential disadvantages of each type of performance testing.

Overview

Performance testing is a generic term that can refer to many different types of performance-related testing, each of which addresses a specific problem area and provides its own benefits, risks, and challenges.

This chapter defines, describes, and outlines the benefits and project risks associated with several common types or categories of performance-related testing. Using this chapter, you will be able to overcome the frequent misuse and misunderstanding of many of these terms even within established teams.

How to Use This Chapter

Use this chapter to understand various types of performance-related testing. This will help your team decide which types of performance-related testing are most likely to add value to a given project based on current risks, concerns, or testing results. To get the most from this chapter:

- Use the "Key Types of Performance Testing" section to make a more informed decision about which type of testing is most relevant to your specific concerns, and to balance the trade-offs between different test types.

- Use the "Summary Matrix of Benefits by Key Performance Test Types" section to ensure that you consider not only the benefits of a particular type of tests, but also the challenges and areas of concern that are likely to not be addressed adequately by that type of performance test.

- Use the "Additional Concepts / Terms" section to become more aware of additional types of performance testing that may add value to your project, and to improve your ability to engage in conversations about performance testing with people outside of your specific context.

Performance Testing

Performance testing is defined as the technical investigation done to determine or validate the speed, scalability, and/or stability characteristics of the product under test. Performance-related activities, such as testing and tuning, are concerned with achieving response times, throughput, and resource-utilization levels that meet the performance objectives for the application under test. Because performance testing is a general term that covers all of its various subsets, every value and benefit listed under other performance test types in this chapter can also be considered a potential benefit of performance testing in general.

Key Types of Performance Testing

The following are the most common types of performance testing for Web applications.

Term	Purpose	Notes
Performance test	To determine or validate speed, scalability, and/or stability.	A performance test is a technical investigation done to determine or validate the responsiveness, speed, scalability, and/or stability characteristics of the product under test.

Term	Purpose	Notes
Load test	To verify application behavior under normal and peak load conditions.	Load testing is conducted to verify that your application can meet your desired performance objectives; these performance objectives are often specified in a service level agreement (SLA). A load test enables you to measure response times, throughput rates, and resource-utilization levels, and to identify your application's breaking point, assuming that the breaking point occurs below the peak load condition. Endurance testing is a subset of load testing. An *endurance test* is a type of performance test focused on determining or validating the performance characteristics of the product under test when subjected to workload models and load volumes anticipated during production operations over an extended period of time. Endurance testing may be used to calculate Mean Time Between Failure (MTBF), Mean Time To Failure (MTTF), and similar metrics.
Stress test	To determine or validate an application's behavior when it is pushed beyond normal or peak load conditions.	The goal of stress testing is to reveal application bugs that surface only under high load conditions. These bugs can include such things as synchronization issues, race conditions, and memory leaks. Stress testing enables you to identify your application's weak points, and shows how the application behaves under extreme load conditions. Spike testing is a subset of stress testing. A *spike test* is a type of performance test focused on determining or validating the performance characteristics of the product under test when subjected to workload models and load volumes that repeatedly increase beyond anticipated production operations for short periods of time.
Capacity test	To determine how many users and/or transactions a given system will support and still meet performance goals.	Capacity testing is conducted in conjunction with capacity planning, which you use to plan for future growth, such as an increased user base or increased volume of data. For example, to accommodate future loads, you need to know how many additional resources (such as processor capacity, memory usage, disk capacity, or network bandwidth) are necessary to support future usage levels. Capacity testing helps you to identify a scaling strategy in order to determine whether you should scale up or scale out.

The most common performance concerns related to Web applications are "Will it be fast enough?", "Will it support all of my clients?", "What happens if something goes wrong?", and "What do I need to plan for when I get more customers?". In casual conversation, most people associate "fast enough" with performance testing, "accommodate the current/expected user base" with load testing, "something going wrong" with stress testing, and "planning for future growth" with capacity testing. Collectively, these risks form the basis for the four key types of performance tests for Web applications.

Summary Matrix of Benefits by Key Performance Test Types

Term	Benefits	Challenges and Areas Not Addressed
Performance test	• Determines the speed, scalability and stability characteristics of an application, thereby providing an input to making sound business decisions. • Focuses on determining if the user of the system will be satisfied with the performance characteristics of the application. • Identifies mismatches between performance-related expectations and reality. • Supports tuning, capacity planning, and optimization efforts.	• May not detect some functional defects that only appear under load. • If not carefully designed and validated, may only be indicative of performance characteristics in a very small number of production scenarios. • Unless tests are conducted on the production hardware, from the same machines the users will be using, there will always be a degree of uncertainty in the results.
Load test	• Determines the throughput required to support the anticipated peak production load. • Determines the adequacy of a hardware environment. • Evaluates the adequacy of a load balancer. • Detects concurrency issues. • Detects functionality errors under load. • Collects data for scalability and capacity-planning purposes. • Helps to determine how many users the application can handle before performance is compromised. • Helps to determine how much load the hardware can handle before resource utilization limits are exceeded.	• Is not designed to primarily focus on speed of response. • Results should only be used for comparison with other related load tests.

Term	Benefits	Challenges and Areas Not Addressed
Stress test	• Determines if data can be corrupted by overstressing the system. • Provides an estimate of how far beyond the target load an application can go before causing failures and errors in addition to slowness. • Allows you to establish application-monitoring triggers to warn of impending failures. • Ensures that security vulnerabilities are not opened up by stressful conditions. • Determines the side effects of common hardware or supporting application failures. • Helps to determine what kinds of failures are most valuable to plan for.	• Because stress tests are unrealistic by design, some stakeholders may dismiss test results. • It is often difficult to know how much stress is worth applying. • It is possible to cause application and/or network failures that may result in significant disruption if not isolated to the test environment.
Capacity test	• Provides information about how workload can be handled to meet business requirements. • Provides actual data that capacity planners can use to validate or ehance their models and/or predictions. • Enables you to conduct various tests to compare capacity-planning models and/or predictions. • Determines the current usage and capacity of the existing system to aid in capacity planning. • Provides the usage and capacity trends of the existing system to aid in capacity planning	• Capacity model validation tests are complex to create. • Not all aspects of a capacity-planning model can be validated through testing at a time when those aspects would provide the most value.

Although the potential benefits far outweigh the challenges related to performance testing, uncertainty over the relevance of the resulting data — based on the sheer impossibility of testing all of the reasonable combinations of variables, scenarios and situations — makes some organizations question the value of conducting performance testing at all. In practice, however, the likelihood of catastrophic performance failures occurring in a system that has been through reasonable (not even rigorous) performance testing is dramatically reduced, particularly if the performance tests are used to help determine what to monitor in production so that the team will get early warning signs if the application starts drifting toward a significant performance-related failure.

Additional Concepts / Terms

You will often see or hear the following terms when conducting performance testing. Some of these terms may be common in your organization, industry, or peer network, while others may not. These terms and concepts have been included because they are used frequently enough, and cause enough confusion, to make them worth knowing.

Term	Notes
Component test	A *component test* is any performance test that targets an architectural component of the application. Commonly tested components include servers, databases, networks, firewalls, clients, and storage devices.
Investigation	*Investigation* is an activity based on collecting information related to the speed, scalability, and/or stability characteristics of the product under test that may have value in determining or improving product quality. Investigation is frequently employed to prove or disprove hypotheses regarding the root cause of one or more observed performance issues.
Smoke test	A *smoke test* is the initial run of a performance test to see if your application can perform its operations under a normal load.
Unit test	In the context of performance testing, a *unit test* is any test that targets a module of code where that module is any logical subset of the entire existing code base of the application, with a focus on performance characteristics. Commonly tested modules include functions, procedures, routines, objects, methods, and classes. Performance unit tests are frequently created and conducted by the developer who wrote the module of code being tested.
Validation test	A *validation test* compares the speed, scalability, and/or stability characteristics of the product under test against the expectations that have been set or presumed for that product.

Summary

Performance testing is a broad and complex activity that can take many forms, address many risks, and provide a wide range of value to an organization.

It is important to understand the different performance test types in order to reduce risks, minimize cost, and know when to apply the appropriate test over the course of a given performance-testing project. To apply different test types over the course of a performance test, you need to evaluate the following key points:

- The objectives of the performance test.
- The context of the performance test; for example, the resources involved, cost, and potential return on the testing effort.

3

Risks Addressed Through Performance Testing

Objectives

- Understand how speed, scalability, and stability are viewed from a performance-testing perspective.
- Learn how performance testing can be used to mitigate risks related to speed, scalability, and stability.
- Learn about the aspects of these risks that performance testing does not adequately address.

Overview

Performance testing is indispensable for managing certain significant business risks. For example, if your Web site cannot handle the volume of traffic it receives, your customers will shop somewhere else. Beyond identifying the obvious risks, performance testing can be a useful way of detecting many other potential problems. While performance testing does not replace other types of testing, it can reveal information relevant to usability, functionality, security, and corporate image that is difficult to obtain in other ways.

Many businesses and performance testers find it valuable to think of the risks that performance testing can address in terms of three categories: speed, scalability, and stability.

How to Use This Chapter

Use this chapter to learn about typical performance risks, the performance test types related to those risks, and proven strategies to mitigate those risks. To get the most from this chapter:

- Use the "Summary Matrix" section to understand the different types of tests and the risks they can mitigate.
- Use the various risk type sections to understand related strategies that can help you determine the best testing approach for your particular situation.

Summary Matrix of Risks Addressed by Performance Testing Types

Performance test type	Risk(s) addressed
Capacity	• Is system capacity meeting business volume under both normal and peak load conditions?
Component	• Is this component meeting expectations? • Is this component reasonably well optimized? • Is the observed performance issue caused by this component?
Endurance	• Will performance be consistent over time? • Are there slowly growing problems that have not yet been detected? • Is there external interference that was not accounted for?
Investigation	• Which way is performance trending over time? • To what should I compare future tests?
Load	• How many users can the application handle before undesirable behavior occurs when the application is subjected to a particular workload? • How much data can my database/file server handle? • Are the network components adequate?
Smoke	• Is this build/configuration ready for additional performance testing? • What type of performance testing should I conduct next? • Does this build exhibit better or worse performance than the last one?
Spike	• What happens if the production load exceeds the anticipated peak load? • What kinds of failures should we plan for? • What indicators should we look for?
Stress	• What happens if the production load exceeds the anticipated load? • What kinds of failures should we plan for? • What indicators should we look for in order to intervene prior to failure?
Unit	• Is this segment of code reasonably efficient? • Did I stay within my performance budgets? • Is this code performing as anticipated under load?
Validation	• Does the application meet the goals and requirements? • Is this version faster or slower than the last one? • Will I be in violation of my contract/Service Level Agreement (SLA) if I release?

Risks	Performance test types									
	Capacity	Component	Endurance	Investigation	Load	Smoke	Spike	Stress	Unit	Validation
Speed-related risks										
User satisfaction			X	X	X			X		X
Synchronicity		X	X	X	X		X	X	X	
Service Level Agreement (SLA) violation			X	X	X					X
Response time trend		X	X	X	X	X			X	
Configuration		X	X	X	X	X		X		X
Consistency		X	X	X	X				X	X
Scalability-related risks										
Capacity	X	X	X	X	X					X
Volume	X	X	X	X	X					X
SLA violation			X	X	X					X
Optimization	X	X		X					X	
Efficiency	X	X		X					X	
Future growth	X	X		X	X					X
Resource consumption	X	X	X	X	X	X	X	X	X	X
Hardware / environment	X	X	X	X	X		X	X		X
Service Level Agreement (SLA) violation	X	X	X	X	X					X
Stability-related risks										
Reliability		X	X	X	X		X	X	X	
Robustness		X	X	X	X		X	X	X	
Hardware / environment			X	X	X		X	X		X
Failure mode		X	X	X	X		X	X	X	X
Slow leak		X	X	X	X				X	
Service Level Agreement (SLA) violation		X	X	X	X		X	X	X	X
Recovery		X		X			X	X	X	X
Data accuracy and security		X	X	X	X		X	X	X	X
Interfaces		X	X	X	X			X	X	X

Speed-Related Risks

Speed-related risks are not confined to end-user satisfaction, although that is what most people think of first. Speed is also a factor in certain business- and data-related risks. Some of the most common speed-related risks that performance testing can address include:

- Is the application fast enough to satisfy end users?
- Is the business able to process and utilize data collected by the application before that data becomes outdated? (For example, end-of-month reports are due within 24 hours of the close of business on the last day of the month, but it takes the application 48 hours to process the data.)
- Is the application capable of presenting the most current information (e.g., stock quotes) to its users?
- Is a Web Service responding within the maximum expected response time before an error is thrown?

Speed-Related Risk-Mitigation Strategies

The following strategies are valuable in mitigating speed-related risks:

- Ensure that your performance requirements and goals represent the needs and desires of your users, not someone else's.
- Compare your speed measurements against previous versions and competing applications.
- Design load tests that replicate actual workload at both normal and anticipated peak times.
- Conduct performance testing with data types, distributions, and volumes similar to those used in business operations during actual production (e.g., number of products, orders in pending status, size of user base). You can allow data to accumulate in databases and file servers, or additionally create the data volume, before load test execution.
- Use performance test results to help stakeholders make informed architecture and business decisions.
- Solicit representative feedback about users' satisfaction with the system while it is under peak expected load.
- Include time-critical transactions in your performance tests.
- Ensure that at least some of your performance tests are conducted while periodic system processes are executing (e.g., downloading virus-definition updates, or during weekly backups).

- Measure speed under various conditions, load levels, and scenario mixes. (Users value consistent speed.)
- Validate that all of the correct data was displayed and saved during your performance test. (For example, a user updates information, but the confirmation screen still displays the old information because the transaction has not completed writing to the database.)

Scalability-Related Risks

Scalability risks concern not only the number of users an application can support, but also the volume of data the application can contain and process, as well as the ability to identify when an application is approaching capacity. Common scalability risks that can be addressed via performance testing include:

- Can the application provide consistent and acceptable response times for the entire user base?
- Can the application store all of the data that will be collected over the life of the application?
- Are there warning signs to indicate that the application is approaching peak capacity?
- Will the application still be secure under heavy usage?
- Will functionality be compromised under heavy usage?
- Can the application withstand unanticipated peak loads?

Scalability-Related Risk-Mitigation Strategies

The following strategies are valuable in mitigating scalability-related risks:

- Compare measured speeds under various loads. (Keep in mind that the end user does not know or care how many other people are using the application at the same time that he/she is.)
- Design load tests that replicate actual workload at both normal and anticipated peak times.
- Conduct performance testing with data types, distributions, and volumes similar to those used in business operations during actual production (e.g., number of products, orders in pending status, size of user base). You can allow data to accumulate in databases and file servers, or additionally create the data volume, before load test execution.
- Use performance test results to help stakeholders make informed architecture and business decisions.

- Work with more meaningful performance tests that map to the real-world requirements.

- When you find a scalability limit, incrementally reduce the load and retest to help you identify a metric that can serve as a reliable indicator that the application is approaching that limit in enough time for you to apply countermeasures.

- Validate the functional accuracy of the application under various loads by checking database entries created or validating content returned in response to particular user requests.

- Conduct performance tests beyond expected peak loads and observe behavior by having representative users and stakeholders access the application manually during and after the performance test.

Stability-Related Risks

Stability is a blanket term that encompasses such areas as reliability, uptime, and recoverability. Although stability risks are commonly addressed with high-load, endurance, and stress tests, stability issues are sometimes detected during the most basic performance tests. Some common stability risks addressed by means of performance testing include:

- Can the application run for long periods of time without data corruption, slow-down, or servers needing to be rebooted?

- If the application does go down unexpectedly, what happens to partially completed transactions?

- When the application comes back online after scheduled or unscheduled downtime, will users still be able to see/do everything they expect?

- When the application comes back online after unscheduled downtime, does it resume at the correct point? In particular, does it not attempt to resume cancelled transactions?

- Can combinations of errors or repeated functional errors cause a system crash?

- Are there any transactions that cause system-wide side effects?

- Can one leg of the load-balanced environment be taken down and still provide uninterrupted service to users?

- Can the system be patched or updated without taking it down?

Stability-Related Risk-Mitigation Strategies

The following strategies are valuable in mitigating stability-related risks:

- Make time for realistic endurance tests.
- Conduct stress testing with the key scenarios. Work with key performance indicators (network, disk, processor, memory) and business indicators such as number of orders lost, user login failures, and so on.
- Conduct stress testing with data feeds that replicate similar business operations as in an actual production environment (e.g., number of products, orders in pending status, size of user base). You can allow data to accumulate in databases and file servers, or additionally create the data volume, before stress test execution. This will allow you to replicate critical errors such as database or application deadlocks and other stress failure patterns.
- Take a server offline during a test and observe functional, performance, and data-integrity behaviors of the remaining systems.
- Execute identical tests immediately before and after a system reboot. Compare the results. You can use an identical approach for recycling services or processes.
- Include error or exception cases in your performance test scenarios (for example, users trying to log on with improper credentials).
- Apply a patch to the system during a performance test.
- Force a backup and/or virus definition update during a performance test.

Summary

Almost all application- and business-related risks can be addressed through performance testing, including user satisfaction and the application's ability to achieve business goals.

Generally, the risks that performance testing addresses are categorized in terms of speed, scalability, and stability. Speed is typically an end-user concern, scalability is a business concern, and stability is a technical or maintenance concern.

Identifying project-related risks and the associated mitigation strategies where performance testing can be employed is almost universally viewed as a valuable and time-saving practice.

Part II

Exemplar Performance Testing Approaches

In this part:

- Web Application Performance Testing Core Activities
- Coordinating Performance Testing With an Iteration-Based Process
- Managing an Agile Performance Test Cycle
- Managing the Performance Test Cycle in a Regulated (CMMI) Environment

4

Web Application Performance Testing Core Activities

Objectives

- Learn the seven core activities that are integral to the majority of performance-testing projects.
- Understand the seven core activities in sufficient detail to identify how your tasks and processes map to these activities.
- Understand various performance-testing approaches that can be built around the core activities.

Overview

This chapter provides a high-level introduction to the most common core activities involved in performance-testing your applications and the systems that support those applications. Performance testing is a complex activity that cannot effectively be shaped into a "one-size-fits-all" or even a "one-size-fits-most" approach. Projects, environments, business drivers, acceptance criteria, technologies, timelines, legal implications, and available skills and tools simply make any notion of a common, universal approach unrealistic.

That said, there are some activities that are part of nearly all project-level performance-testing efforts. These activities may occur at different times, be called different things, have different degrees of focus, and be conducted either implicitly or explicitly, but when all is said and done, it is quite rare when a performance-testing project does not involve at least making a decision around the seven core activities identified and referenced throughout this guide. These seven core activities do not in themselves constitute an approach to performance testing; rather, they represent the foundation upon which an approach can be built that is appropriate for your project.

How to Use This Chapter

Use this chapter to understand the core activities of performance testing and what these activities accomplish. To get the most from this chapter:

- Use the "Summary Table of Core Performance Activities" section to get an overview of the core activities of performance testing, and as quick reference guide for you and your team.

- Use the various Activity sections to understand the details of the most critical performance-testing tasks, as well as considerations for each activity.

Overview of Activities

The following sections discuss the seven activities that most commonly occur across successful performance-testing projects. The key to effectively implementing these activities is not when you conduct them, what you call them, whether or not they overlap, or the iteration pattern among them, but rather that you understand and carefully consider the concepts, applying them in the manner that is most valuable to your own project context.

Starting with at least a cursory knowledge of the project context, most teams begin identifying the test environment and the performance acceptance criteria more or less in parallel. This is due to the fact that all of the remaining activities are affected by the information gathered in activities 1 and 2. Generally, you will revisit these activities periodically as you and your team learn more about the application, its users, its features, and any performance-related risks it might have.

Once you have a good enough understanding of the project context, the test environment, and the performance acceptance criteria, you will begin planning and designing performance tests and configuring the test environment with the tools needed to conduct the kinds of performance tests and collect the kinds of data that you currently anticipate needing, as described in activities 3 and 4. Once again, in most cases you will revisit these activities periodically as more information becomes available.

With at least the relevant aspects of activities 1 through 4 accomplished, most teams will move into an iterative test cycle (activities 5-7) where designed tests are implemented by using some type of load-generation tool, the implemented tests are executed, and the results of those tests are analyzed and reported in terms of their relation to the components and features available to test at that time.

To the degree that performance testing begins before the system or application to be tested has been completed, there is a naturally iterative cycle that results from testing features and components as they become available and continually gaining more information about the application, its users, its features, and any performance-related risks that present themselves via testing.

Summary Table of Core Performance-Testing Activities

The following table summarizes the seven core performance-testing activities along with the most common input and output for each activity. Note that project context is not listed, although it is a critical input item for each activity.

Activity	Input	Output
Activity 1. Identify the Test Environment	• Logical and physical production architecture • Logical and physical test architecture • Available tools	• Comparison of test and production environments • Environment-related concerns • Determination of whether additional tools are required
Activity 2. Identify Performance Acceptance Criteria	• Client expectations • Risks to be mitigated • Business requirements • Contractual obligations	• Performance-testing success criteria • Performance goals and requirements • Key areas of investigation • Key performance indicators • Key business indicators
Activity 3. Plan and Design Tests	• Available application features and/or components • Application usage scenarios • Unit tests • Performance acceptance criteria	• Conceptual strategy • Test execution prerequisites • Tools and resources required • Application usage models to be simulated • Test data required to implement tests • Tests ready to be implemented
Activity 4. Configure the Test Environment	• Conceptual strategy • Available tools • Designed tests	• Configured load-generation and resource-monitoring tools • Environment ready for performance testing
Activity 5. Implement the Test Design	• Conceptual strategy • Available tools/environment • Available application features and/or components • Designed tests	• Validated, executable tests • Validated resource monitoring • Validated data collection
Activity 6. Execute the Test	• Task execution plan • Available tools/environment • Available application features and/or components • Validated, executable tests	• Test execution results
Activity 7. Analyze Results, Report, and Retest	• Task execution results • Performance acceptance criteria • Risks, concerns, and issues	• Results analysis • Recommendations • Reports

Core Performance-Testing Activities Walkthrough

The seven core performance-testing activities can be summarized as follows.

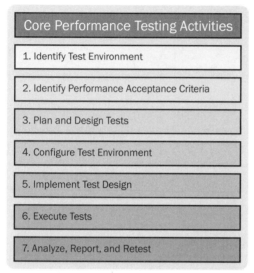

Figure 4.1 *Core Performance Testing Activities*

1. **Activity 1. Identify the Test Environment.** Identify the physical test environment and the production environment as well as the tools and resources available to the test team. The physical environment includes hardware, software, and network configurations. Having a thorough understanding of the entire test environment at the outset enables more efficient test design and planning and helps you identify testing challenges early in the project. In some situations, this process must be revisited periodically throughout the project's life cycle.

2. **Activity 2. Identify Performance Acceptance Criteria.** Identify the response time, throughput, and resource utilization goals and constraints. In general, response time is a user concern, throughput is a business concern, and resource utilization is a system concern. Additionally, identify project success criteria that may not be captured by those goals and constraints; for example, using performance tests to evaluate what combination of configuration settings will result in the most desirable performance characteristics.

3. **Activity 3. Plan and Design Tests.** Identify key scenarios, determine variability among representative users and how to simulate that variability, define test data, and establish metrics to be collected. Consolidate this information into one or more models of system usage to be implemented, executed, and analyzed.

4. **Activity 4. Configure the Test Environment.** Prepare the test environment, tools, and resources necessary to execute each strategy as features and components become available for test. Ensure that the test environment is instrumented for resource monitoring as necessary.

5. **Activity 5. Implement the Test Design.** Develop the performance tests in accordance with the test design.

6. **Activity 6. Execute the Test.** Run and monitor your tests. Validate the tests, test data, and results collection. Execute validated tests for analysis while monitoring the test and the test environment.

7. **Activity 7. Analyze Results, Report, and Retest.** Consolidate and share results data. Analyze the data both individually and as a cross-functional team. Reprioritize the remaining tests and re-execute them as needed. When all of the metric values are within accepted limits, none of the set thresholds have been violated, and all of the desired information has been collected, you have finished testing that particular scenario on that particular configuration.

Activity 1. Identify the Test Environment

The environment in which your performance tests will be executed, along with the tools and associated hardware necessary to execute the performance tests, constitute the test environment. Under ideal conditions, if the goal is to determine the performance characteristics of the application in production, the test environment is an exact replica of the production environment but with the addition of load-generation and resource-monitoring tools. Exact replicas of production environments are uncommon.

The degree of similarity between the hardware, software, and network configuration of the application under test conditions and under actual production conditions is often a significant consideration when deciding what performance tests to conduct and what size loads to test. It is important to remember that it is not only the physical and software environments that impact performance testing, but also the objectives of the test itself. Often, performance tests are applied against a proposed new hardware infrastructure to validate the supposition that the new hardware will address existing performance concerns.

The key factor in identifying your test environment is to completely understand the similarities and differences between the test and production environments. Some critical factors to consider are:

- Hardware
  - Configurations
  - Machine hardware (processor, RAM, etc.)

- Network
  - Network architecture and end-user location
  - Load-balancing implications
  - Cluster and Domain Name System (DNS) configurations
- Tools
  - Load-generation tool limitations
  - Environmental impact of monitoring tools
- Software
  - Other software installed or running in shared or virtual environments
  - Software license constraints or differences
  - Storage capacity and seed data volume
  - Logging levels
- External factors
  - Volume and type of additional traffic on the network
  - Scheduled or batch processes, updates, or backups
  - Interactions with other systems

Considerations

Consider the following key points when characterizing the test environment:

- Although few performance testers install, configure, and administrate the application being tested, it is beneficial for the testers to have access to the servers and software, or to the administrators who do.
- Identify the amount and type of data the application must be seeded with to emulate real-world conditions.
- Identify critical system components. Do any of the system components have known performance concerns? Are there any integration points that are beyond your control for testing?
- Get to know the IT staff. You will likely need their support to perform tasks such as monitoring overall network traffic and configuring your load-generation tool to simulate a realistic number of Internet Protocol (IP) addresses.
- Check the configuration of load balancers.
- Validate name resolution with DNS. This may account for significant latency when opening database connections.
- Validate that firewalls, DNS, routing, and so on treat the generated load similarly to a load that would typically be encountered in a production environment.
- It is often appropriate to have systems administrators set up resource-monitoring software, diagnostic tools, and other utilities in the test environment.

Activity 2. Identify Performance Acceptance Criteria

It generally makes sense to start identifying, or at least estimating, the desired performance characteristics of the application early in the development life cycle. This can be accomplished most simply by noting the performance characteristics that your users and stakeholders equate with good performance. The notes can be quantified at a later time.

Classes of characteristics that frequently correlate to a user's or stakeholder's satisfaction typically include:

- **Response time.** For example, the product catalog must be displayed in less than three seconds.
- **Throughput.** For example, the system must support 25 book orders per second.
- **Resource utilization.** For example, processor utilization is not more than 75 percent. Other important resources that need to be considered for setting objectives are memory, disk input/output (I/O), and network I/O.

Considerations

Consider the following key points when identifying performance criteria:

- Business requirements
- User expectations
- Contractual obligations
- Regulatory compliance criteria and industry standards
- Service Level Agreements (SLAs)
- Resource utilization targets
- Various and diverse, realistic workload models
- The entire range of anticipated load conditions
- Conditions of system stress
- Entire scenarios and component activities
- Key performance indicators
- Previous releases of the application
- Competitor's applications
- Optimization objectives
- Safety factors, room for growth, and scalability
- Schedule, staffing, budget, resources, and other priorities

Activity 3. Plan and Design Tests

Planning and designing performance tests involves identifying key usage scenarios, determining appropriate variability across users, identifying and generating test data, and specifying the metrics to be collected. Ultimately, these items will provide the foundation for workloads and workload profiles.

When designing and planning tests with the intention of characterizing production performance, your goal should be to create real-world simulations in order to provide reliable data that will enable your organization to make informed business decisions. Real-world test designs will significantly increase the relevancy and usefulness of results data.

Key usage scenarios for the application typically surface during the process of identifying the desired performance characteristics of the application. If this is not the case for your test project, you will need to explicitly determine the usage scenarios that are the most valuable to script. Consider the following when identifying key usage scenarios:

- Contractually obligated usage scenario(s)
- Usage scenarios implied or mandated by performance-testing goals and objectives
- Most common usage scenario(s)
- Business-critical usage scenario(s)
- Performance-intensive usage scenario(s)
- Usage scenarios of technical concern
- Usage scenarios of stakeholder concern
- High-visibility usage scenarios

When identified, captured, and reported correctly, metrics provide information about how your application's performance compares to your desired performance characteristics. In addition, metrics can help you identify problem areas and bottlenecks within your application.

It is useful to identify the metrics related to the performance acceptance criteria during test design so that the method of collecting those metrics can be integrated into the tests when implementing the test design. When identifying metrics, use either specific desired characteristics or indicators that are directly or indirectly related to those characteristics.

Considerations

Consider the following key points when planning and designing tests:

- Realistic test designs are sensitive to dependencies outside the control of the system, such as humans, network activity, and other systems interacting with the application.

- Realistic test designs are based on what you expect to find in real-world use, not theories or projections.
- Realistic test designs produce more credible results and thus enhance the value of performance testing.
- Component-level performance tests are integral parts of realistic testing.
- Realistic test designs can be more costly and time-consuming to implement, but they provide far more accuracy for the business and stakeholders.
- Extrapolating performance results from unrealistic tests can create damaging in-accuracies as the system scope increases, and frequently lead to poor decisions.
- Involve the developers and administrators in the process of determining which metrics are likely to add value and which method best integrates the capturing of those metrics into the test.
- Beware of allowing your tools to influence your test design. Better tests almost always result from designing tests on the assumption that they can be executed and then adapting the test or the tool when that assumption is proven false, rather than by *not* designing particular tests based on the assumption that you do not have access to a tool to execute the test.

Realistic test designs include:

- Realistic simulations of user delays and think times, which are crucial to the accuracy of the test.
- User abandonment, if users are likely to abandon a task for any reason.
- Common user errors.

Activity 4. Configure the Test Environment

Preparing the test environment, tools, and resources for test design implementation and test execution prior to features and components becoming available for test can significantly increase the amount of testing that can be accomplished during the time those features and components are available.

Load-generation and application-monitoring tools are almost never as easy to get up and running as one expects. Whether issues arise from setting up isolated network environments, procuring hardware, coordinating a dedicated bank of IP addresses for IP spoofing, or version compatibility between monitoring software and server operating systems, issues always seem to arise from somewhere. Start early, to ensure that issues are resolved before you begin testing.

Additionally, plan to periodically reconfigure, update, add to, or otherwise enhance your load-generation environment and associated tools throughout the project. Even if the application under test stays the same and the load-generation tool is working properly, it is likely that the metrics you want to collect will change. This frequently implies some degree of change to, or addition of, monitoring tools.

Considerations

Consider the following key points when configuring the test environment:

- Determine how much load you can generate before the load generators reach a bottleneck. Typically, load generators encounter bottlenecks first in memory and then in the processor.

- Although it may seem like a commonsense practice, it is important to verify that system clocks are synchronized on all of the machines from which resource data will be collected. Doing so can save you significant time and prevent you from having to dispose of the data entirely and repeat the tests after synchronizing the system clocks.

- Validate the accuracy of load test execution against hardware components such as switches and network cards. For example, ensure the correct full-duplex mode operation and correct emulation of user latency and bandwidth.

- Validate the accuracy of load test execution related to server clusters in load-balanced configuration. Consider using load-testing techniques to avoid affinity of clients to servers due to their using the same IP address. Most load-generation tools offer the ability to simulate usage of different IP addresses across load-test generators.

- Monitor resource utilization (CPU, network, memory, disk and transactions per time) across servers in the load-balanced configuration during a load test to validate that the load is distributed.

Activity 5. Implement the Test Design

The details of creating an executable performance test are extremely tool-specific. Regardless of the tool that you are using, creating a performance test typically involves scripting a single usage scenario and then enhancing that scenario and combining it with other scenarios to ultimately represent a complete workload model.

Load-generation tools inevitably lag behind evolving technologies and practices. Tool creators can only build in support for the most prominent technologies and, even then, these have to become prominent before the support can be built. This often means that the biggest challenge involved in a performance-testing project is getting your first relatively realistic test implemented with users generally being simulated in such a way that the application under test cannot legitimately tell the difference between the simulated users and real users. Plan for this and do not be surprised when it takes significantly longer than expected to get it all working smoothly.

Considerations

Consider the following key points when implementing the test design:

- Ensure that test data feeds are implemented correctly. Test data feeds are data repositories in the form of databases, text files, in-memory variables, or spreadsheets that are used to simulate parameter replacement during a load test. For example, even if the application database test repository contains the full production set, your load test might only need to simulate a subset of products being bought by users due to a scenario involving, for example, a new product or marketing campaign. Test data feeds may be a subset of production data repositories.

- Ensure that application data feeds are implemented correctly in the database and other application components. Application data feeds are data repositories, such as product or order databases, that are consumed by the application being tested. The key user scenarios, run by the load test scripts may consume a subset of this data.

- Ensure that validation of transactions is implemented correctly. Many transactions are reported successful by the Web server, but they fail to complete correctly. Examples of validation are, database entries inserted with correct number of rows, product information being returned, correct content returned in html data to the clients etc.

- Ensure hidden fields or other special data are handled correctly. This refers to data returned by Web server that needs to be resubmitted in subsequent request, like session IDs or product ID that needs to be incremented before passing it to the next request.

- Validate the monitoring of key performance indicators (KPIs).

- Add pertinent indicators to facilitate articulating business performance.

- If the request accepts parameters, ensure that the parameter data is populated properly with variables and/or unique data to avoid any server-side caching.

- If the tool does not do so automatically, consider adding a wrapper around the requests in the test script in order to measure the request response time.

- It is generally worth taking the time to make the script match your designed test, rather than changing the designed test to save scripting time.

- Significant value can be gained from evaluating the output data collected from executed tests against expectations in order to test or validate script development.

Activity 6. Execute the Test

Executing tests is what most people envision when they think about performance testing. It makes sense that the process, flow, and technical details of test execution are extremely dependent on your tools, environment, and project context. Even so, there are some fairly universal tasks and considerations that need to be kept in mind when executing tests.

Much of the performance testing–related training available today treats test execution as little more than starting a test and monitoring it to ensure that the test appears to be running as expected. In reality, this activity is significantly more complex than just clicking a button and monitoring machines.

Test execution can be viewed as a combination of the following sub-tasks:

1. Coordinate test execution and monitoring with the team.
2. Validate tests, configurations, and the state of the environments and data.
3. Begin test execution.
4. While the test is running, monitor and validate scripts, systems, and data.
5. Upon test completion, quickly review the results for obvious indications that the test was flawed.
6. Archive the tests, test data, results, and other information necessary to repeat the test later if needed.
7. Log start and end times, the name of the result data, and so on. This will allow you to identify your data sequentially after your test is done.

As you prepare to begin test execution, it is worth taking the time to double-check the following items:

- Validate that the test environment matches the configuration that you were expecting and/or designed your test for.
- Ensure that both the test and the test environment are correctly configured for metrics collection.
- Before running the real test, execute a quick smoke test to make sure that the test script and remote performance counters are working correctly. In the context of performance testing, a *smoke test* is designed to determine if your application can successfully perform all of its operations under a normal load condition for a short time.
- Reset the system (unless your scenario calls for doing otherwise) and start a formal test execution.
- Make sure that the test scripts' execution represents the workload model you want to simulate.
- Make sure that the test is configured to collect the key performance and business indicators of interest at this time.

Considerations

Consider the following key points when executing the test:

- Validate test executions for data updates, such as orders in the database that have been completed.

- Validate if the load-test script is using the correct data values, such as product and order identifiers, in order to realistically simulate the business scenario.

- Whenever possible, limit test execution cycles to one to two days each. Review and reprioritize after each cycle.

- If at all possible, execute every test three times. Note that the results of first-time tests can be affected by loading Dynamic-Link Libraries (DLLs), populating server-side caches, or initializing scripts and other resources required by the code under test. If the results of the second and third iterations are not highly similar, execute the test again. Try to determine what factors account for the difference.

- Observe your test during execution and pay close attention to any behavior you feel is unusual. Your instincts are usually right, or at least valuable indicators.

- No matter how far in advance a test is scheduled, give the team 30-minute and 5-minute warnings before launching the test (or starting the day's testing) if you are using a shared test environment. Additionally, inform the team whenever you are not going to be executing for more than one hour in succession so that you do not impede the completion of their tasks.

- Do not process data, write reports, or draw diagrams on your load-generating machine while generating a load, because this can skew the results of your test.

- Turn off any active virus-scanning on load-generating machines during testing to minimize the likelihood of unintentionally skewing the results of your test.

- While load is being generated, access the system manually from a machine outside of the load-generation environment during test execution so that you can compare your observations with the results data at a later time.

- Remember to simulate ramp-up and cool-down periods appropriately.

- Do not throw away the first iteration because of application script compilation, Web server cache building, or other similar reasons. Instead, measure this iteration separately so that you will know what the first user after a system-wide reboot can expect.

- Test execution is never really finished, but eventually you will reach a point of diminishing returns on a particular test. When you stop obtaining valuable information, move on to other tests.

- If you feel you are not making progress in understanding an observed issue, it may be more efficient to eliminate one or more variables or potential causes and then run the test again.

Activity 7. Analyze Results, Report, and Retest

Managers and stakeholders need more than just the results from various tests — they need conclusions, as well as consolidated data that supports those conclusions. Technical team members also need more than just results — they need analysis, comparisons, and details behind how the results were obtained. Team members of all types get value from performance results being shared more frequently.

Before results can be reported, the data must be analyzed. Consider the following important points when analyzing the data returned by your performance test:

- Analyze the data both individually and as part of a collaborative, cross-functional technical team.

- Analyze the captured data and compare the results against the metric's acceptable or expected level to determine whether the performance of the application being tested shows a trend toward or away from the performance objectives.

- If the test fails, a diagnosis and tuning activity are generally warranted.

- If you fix any bottlenecks, repeat the test to validate the fix.

- Performance-testing results will often enable the team to analyze components at a deep level and correlate the information back to the real world with proper test design and usage analysis.

- Performance test results should enable informed architecture and business decisions.

- Frequently, the analysis will reveal that, in order to completely understand the results of a particular test, additional metrics will need to be captured during subsequent test-execution cycles.

- Immediately share test results and make raw data available to your entire team.

- Talk to the consumers of the data to validate that the test achieved the desired results and that the data means what you think it means.

- Modify the test to get new, better, or different information if the results do not represent what the test was defined to determine.

- Use current results to set priorities for the next test.

- Collecting metrics frequently produces very large volumes of data. Although it is tempting to reduce the amount of data, always exercise caution when using data-reduction techniques because valuable data can be lost.

Most reports fall into one of the following two categories:

- Technical Reports
  - Description of the test, including workload model and test environment.
  - Easily digestible data with minimal pre-processing.

- Access to the complete data set and test conditions.
- Short statements of observations, concerns, questions, and requests for collaboration.
- Stakeholder Reports
  - Criteria to which the results relate.
  - Intuitive, visual representations of the most relevant data.
  - Brief verbal summaries of the chart or graph in terms of criteria.
  - Intuitive, visual representations of the workload model and test environment.
  - Access to associated technical reports, complete data sets, and test conditions.
  - Summaries of observations, concerns, and recommendations.

The key to effective reporting is to present information of interest to the intended audience in a manner that is quick, simple, and intuitive. The following are some underlying principles for achieving effective reports:

- Report early, report often.
- Report visually.
- Report intuitively.
- Use the right statistics.
- Consolidate data correctly.
- Summarize data effectively.
- Customize for the intended audience.
- Use concise verbal summaries using strong but factual language.
- Make the data available to stakeholders.
- Filter out any unnecessary data.
- If reporting intermediate results, include the priorities, concerns, and blocks for the next several test-execution cycles.

Summary

Performance testing involves a set of common core activities that occur at different stages of projects. Each activity has specific characteristics and tasks to be accomplished. These activities have been found to be present — or at least to have been part of an active, risk-based decision to omit one of the activities — in every deliberate and successful performance-testing project that the authors and reviewers have experienced. It is important to understand each activity in detail and then apply the activities in a way that best fits the project context.

5

Coordinating Performance Testing with an Iteration-Based Process

Objectives

- Learn an approach to coordinating performance testing within an iteration-based process.
- Learn how to detect and solve major issues early in the project.
- Learn how to maximize flexibility without sacrificing control.
- Learn how to provide managers and stakeholders with progress and value indicators.
- Learn how to provide a structure for capturing information that will not noticeably impact the release schedule.
- Learn how to apply an approach that is designed to embrace change, not simply to tolerate it.

Overview

This chapter provides guidance for coordinating performance testing with iteration-based processes that are found in Agile Software Development, Extreme Programming (XP), the Rational Unified Process (RUP), and other sources. The chapter describes the concepts underlying the activities necessary to make performance testing successful within an iterative process, as well as specific, actionable items that you can immediately apply to your project in order to gain a significant return on this investment.

Performance testing is a critical aspect of many software projects because it tests the architectural aspects of the customer experience and provides an indication of overall software quality. Because it is frequently expensive to set up and integrate performance testing, project teams often wait until the end of the project development/test life cycle to do so. The potential side effect to this approach is that when major issues are found near the end of the development life cycle, it becomes much more expensive to resolve them.

The key to working within an iteration-based work cycle is team coordination. For this reason, the performance tester must be able to adapt what he or she measures and analyzes per iteration cycle as circumstances change.

How to Use This Chapter

Use this chapter to understand the activities involved in performance testing in iterative development environments, and their relationship with the core performance-testing activities. Also use this chapter to understand what is accomplished during these activities. To get the most from this chapter:

- Use the "Iterative Performance Testing Activities" section to get an overview of the core activities of performance testing in iterative development environments, and as a quick reference guide for you and your team.
- Use the various activity sections to understand the details of the most critical performance-testing tasks.
- Additionally, use Chapter 4, "Core Activities" to understand the common core activities involved in successful performance-testing projects. This will help you to apply the concepts behind those activities to a particular approach to performance testing.

Introduction to the Approach

When viewed from a linear perspective, the approach starts by examining the software development project as a whole, the reasons why stakeholders have chosen to include performance testing in the project, and the value that performance testing is expected to bring to the project. The results of this examination include the team's view of the success criteria for the performance-testing effort.

Once the success criteria are understood at a high level, an overall strategy is envisioned to guide the general approach to achieving those criteria by summarizing what performance testing activities are anticipated to add the most value at various points during the development life cycle. Those points may include key project deliveries, checkpoints, sprints, iterations, or weekly builds. For the purposes of this chapter, these events are collectively referred to as "performance builds." Frequently, while the strategy is evolving, the performance specialist and/or the team will begin setting up a performance-test environment and a load-generation environment.

With a strategy in mind and the necessary environments in place, the test team draws up plans for major tests or tasks identified for imminent performance builds. When a performance build is delivered, the plan's tasks should be executed in priority sequence (based on all currently available information), appropriately reporting, recording, revising, reprioritizing, adding, and removing tasks and improving the application and the overall plan as the work progresses.

Iterative Performance Testing Activities

This approach can be represented by using the following nine activities:

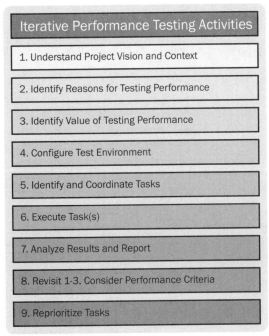

Figure 5.1 *Iterative Performance Testing Activities*

- **Activity 1. Understand the Project Vision and Context.** The outcome of this activity is a shared understanding of the project vision and context.
- **Activity 2. Identify Reasons for Testing Performance.** Explicitly identify the reasons for performance testing.
- **Activity 3. Identify the Value Performance Testing Adds to the Project.** Translate the project- and business-level objectives into specific, identifiable, and manageable performance-testing activities.
- **Activity 4. Configure the Test Environment.** Set up the load-generation tools and the system under test, collectively known as the performance test environment.

- **Activity 5. Identify and Coordinate Tasks.** Prioritize and coordinate support, resources, and schedules to make the tasks efficient and successful.
- **Activity 6. Execute Task(s).** Execute the activities for the current iteration.
- **Activity 7. Analyze Results and Report.** Analyze and share results with the team.
- **Activity 8. Revisit Activities 1-3 and Consider Performance Acceptance Criteria.** Between iterations, ensure that the foundational information has not changed. Integrate new information such as customer feedback and update the strategy as necessary.
- **Activity 9. Reprioritize Tasks.** Based on the test results, new information, and the availability of features and components, reprioritize, add to, or delete tasks from the strategy, and then return to activity 5.

Relationship to Core Performance Testing Activities

The following graphic displays how the seven core activities described in Chapter 4 map to these nine activities:

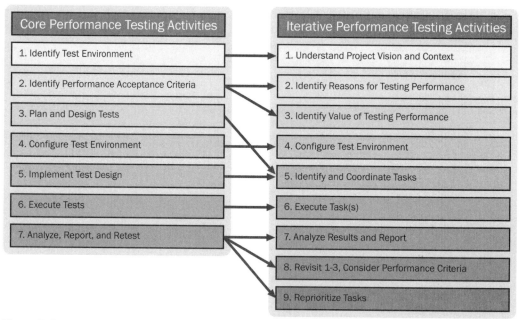

Figure 5.2 *Relationship to Core Performance Testing Activities*

Activity 1. Understand the Project Vision and Context

The project vision and context are the foundation for determining what performance testing activities are necessary and valuable. Because the performance tester is not driving these items, the coordination aspect refers more to team education about the performance implications of the project vision and context, and to identifying areas where future coordination will likely be needed for success.

A critical part of working with an iteration-based process is asking the correct questions, providing the correct value, and performing the correct task related to each step. Although situations can shift or add more questions, values, or tasks, a sample checklist is provided as a starting point for each step.

Checklist

Questions to ask:

- What are the performance implications of the project vision?
- What are the performance implications of the service the application is intended to provide, or what problem are we trying to solve for the customer?
- How does the team envision performance testing as it relates to the project schedule, structure, and available resources?

Value provided:

- Be involved in the product concept.
- Point out any areas of concern immediately.
- Point out assumptions related to available resources, tools, and resource-monitoring instrumentation based on the project vision and context as soon as they arise.

Tasks accomplished:

- Ask the whole team questions and provide answers.
- Determine the team's perception of performance testing.
- Gain a conceptual understanding of the project's critical performance implications.
- Begin to define equipment and/or resources needed for conducting performance testing.
- Understand resource constrains; for example, budget, people, equipment.
- Understand how the team will coordinate.
- Understand how the team will communicate.

Coordinate with:

- Whole team

Activity 2. Identify Reasons for Testing Performance

The underlying reasons for testing performance on a particular project are not always obvious based on the vision and context alone. Project teams generally do not include performance testing as part of the project unless there is some performance-related risk or concern they feel needs to be mitigated. Explicitly identifying these risks and areas of concern is the next fundamental step in determining what specific performance testing activities will add the most value to the project.

Having a full-time performance tester on the team from the start of the project may frequently be a good idea, but it does not happen frequently. Generally, when a performance tester is present at project inception, it means there is a specific, significant risk that the tester is there to address.

Regardless of when a performance tester joins the team, once the project vision and context are understood, it is worth taking the time to verbalize and/or document the overall objectives of the performance-testing effort based on the risks or concerns that the team has. The following checklist should help you to accomplish this step.

Checklist

Questions to ask:

- What risk(s) is performance testing intended to mitigate for this project?
- Are there specific contractual, compliance, or customer performance expectations that are already known to be required?
- What performance concerns relating to this project already exist?

Value provided:

- Be involved in the product concept.
- Point out any areas of concern immediately.
- Point out resource and instrumentation assumptions based on the project vision and context when they arise.
- Guide the process of collecting/determining performance-testing objectives.
- Capture implied usage scenarios of particular performance concerns.
- Capture implied performance goals, requirements, targets, and thresholds as they come up in conversation.

Tasks accomplished:

- Ask the whole team questions and provide answers.
- Determine the project-level objectives for conducting performance testing.
- Refine estimates of equipment and/or resources required for conducting performance testing.

- Identify disconnects between the objectives of the performance-testing effort and the equipment and resources to be made available.
- Capture implied performance goals, requirements, targets, and thresholds to be fleshed out later.
- Capture implied usage scenarios of particular concern to be fleshed out later.

Coordinate with:

- Whole team

Activity 3. Identify the Value Performance Testing Adds to the Project

Using information gained from activities 1 and 2, you can now clarify the value added through performance testing, and convert that value into a conceptual performance-testing strategy. The point is to translate the project- and business-level objectives into specific, identifiable, and manageable performance-testing activities. The co-ordination aspect of this step involves team-wide discussion and agreement on which performance-testing activities are likely to add value or provide valuable information, and if these activities are worth planning for at this time.

Checklist

Questions to ask:

- What performance-testing activities will help achieve the performance-testing objectives?
- What performance-testing activities are needed to validate any contractual, compliance, project, or customer performance criteria or expectations that are known at this time?
- What performance-testing activities will help address currently known performance concerns?

Value provided:

- Ensure team-wide support of performance-testing activities.
- Ensure that the team has adequate warning about performance-testing activities that will require the support of additional team members.
- Determine if resource and instrumentation assumptions are adequate.
- Guide the process of determining how performance-testing objectives will be measured.
- Capture additional implied usage scenarios of particular performance concerns.
- Capture additional implied performance goals, requirements, targets, and thresholds as they come up in conversation.

Tasks accomplished:

- Ask the whole team questions and provide answers.
- Determine a conceptual project-level strategy for determining if the objectives for conducting performance testing have been met.
- Refine estimates of equipment and/or resources required for conducting performance testing.
- Identify disconnects between the objectives of the performance-testing effort and the equipment and resources to be made available.
- Capture additional implied performance goals, requirements, targets, and thresholds to be fleshed out later.
- Capture additional implied usage scenarios of particular concern to be fleshed out later.

Coordinate with:

- Whole team

Activity 4. Configure the Test Environment

With a conceptual strategy in place, prepare the tools and resources in order to execute the strategy as features and components become available for test. Take this step as soon as possible, so that the team has this resource from the beginning.

This step is fairly straightforward. Set up the load-generation tools and the system under test — collectively known as the performance test environment — and ensure that this environment will meet engineering needs. The coordination component of this step typically involves asking managers and administrators to obtain and/or configure equipment and other resources that are not under the direct control of the team or performance tester.

Checklist

Questions to ask:

- Who administrates the performance-testing environment of the application under test?
- Who administrates the load-generation tool/environment?
- Who configures and operates resource monitors for the application under test?
- Is special permission needed prior to generating load of a certain volume?
- Who can reset the application under test?

- What other components require special coordination?
- What security or authentication considerations are there for simulating multiple users?
- What coordination needs to be done to enable the use of recording and/or monitoring software?

Value provided:

- Ensure that the load-generation and performance-test environments are ready when the team needs them.
- Ensure that the entire team knows who to contact for help with performance-testing environment support.
- Ensure that performance testing support staff knows what they are supporting.

Tasks accomplished:

- Performance-test environment configured and ready to begin testing.
- Load-generation environment configured and ready to begin testing.
- Support responsibilities assigned.
- Special permissions, time of day for high load tests, etc., determined.

Coordinate with:

- System administrators
- Network support
- Database administrators
- Infrastructure support
- Managers of those above
- Development team

Activity 5. Identify and Coordinate Tasks

Performance testing tasks do not happen in isolation. The performance specialist needs to work with the team to prioritize and coordinate support, resources, and schedules to make the tasks efficient and successful.

During the pre-iteration planning meeting, look at where the project is now and where you want to be to determine what should and can be done next. When planning for the iteration cycle, the performance tester is driven by the goals that have been determined for this cycle. This step also includes signing up for the activities that will be accomplished during this cycle.

Checklist

Questions to ask:

- What is the performance goal for this cycle?
- Where is the project in terms of the overall project performance goals?
- Has the system achieved all of its performance objectives?
- Has tuning been accomplished since the last iteration?
- What analysis, reports, or retesting will add value during this iteration?
- Who requires pairing in order to do performance testing?
- How much time is available?
- How much time does each task take?
- What is the most critical activity?

Value provided:

- Provide insight on how the overall project is achieving its goal.
- Provide insight on what can be measured and reported on in this cycle.
- Provide insight on any critical issues that may have arisen from the last iteration cycle.
- Make suggestions to other team members.
- Transfer lessons learned as they emerge from the test.
- Pair with developers to improve performance unit testing.
- Help reuse unit tests.
- Help reuse functional tests.

Tasks accomplished:

- Estimate how much work is achievable.
- Determine if anyone needs to be paired out.
- Prioritize achievable work.
- Identify primary and alternate tasks for this cycle.

Coordinate with:

- Managers and stakeholders
- Developers and administrators
- Infrastructure and test environment support
- Users or user representatives

Activity 6. Execute Task(s)

Conduct tasks in one- to two-day segments. See them through to completion, but be willing to take important detours along the way if an opportunity to add additional value presents itself. Step 5 defines what work the team members will sign up for in this iteration. Now it is time to execute the activities for this iteration.

Checklist

Questions to ask:

- Have recent test results or project updates made this task more or less valuable compared to other tests we could be conducting right now?
- What additional team members should be involved with this task?
- Are there other important tasks that can be conducted in parallel with this one?
- Do the preliminary results make sense?
- Is the test providing the data we expected?

Value provided:

- Evaluate algorithm efficiency.
- Monitor resource usage trends.
- Measure response times.
- Collect data for scalability and capacity planning.
- Transfer lessons learned as they emerge from the test.
- Improve performance unit testing by pairing performance testers with developers.
- Help reuse unit tests.
- Help reuse functional tests.

Tasks accomplished:

- Conduct tests.
- Collect data.
- Validate test assumptions and techniques.
- Potentially tune while testing.
- Pair with other team members; this does not mean only working with a developer or tester but can also mean working with a writer to capture his or her understanding of how the system performance works, or working with the customer directly.

Coordinate with:

- Developers and administrators
- Infrastructure and test environment support
- Users or user representatives
- Managers and stakeholders
- Other performance testers who are not on the project

Activity 7. Analyze Results and Report

To keep up with an iterative process, results need to be analyzed and shared quickly. If the analysis is inconclusive, retest at the earliest possible opportunity to give the team maximum time to react to performance issues. As the project is wrapped for final shipping, it is usually worth having a meeting afterward to collect and pass along lessons learned. In most cases it is valuable to have a daily or every-other-day update to share information and coordinate next tasks.

Checklist

Questions to ask:

- Do the preliminary results make sense?
- Is the test providing the data we expected?
- Is the data valuable?
- Are more tests required to derive meaning from the data?
- Is tuning required? If so, do we know what to tune?
- Do the results indicate that there are additional tests that we need to execute that have not been planned for?
- Do the results indicate that any of the tests we are planning to conduct are no longer necessary?
- Have any performance objectives been met?
- Have any performance objectives been rendered obsolete?

Value provided:

- Evaluate algorithm efficiency.
- Monitor resource usage trends.
- Measure response times.
- Collect data for scalability and capacity planning.
- Transfer lessons learned as they emerge from the test.

Tasks accomplished:

- Analyze data collaboratively.
- Determine the meaning of the results.
- Share data with the whole team.
- Import lessons learned into future iteration planning.

Coordinate with:

- Developers and administrators
- Managers and stakeholders
- Users or user representatives
- Other performance testers who are not on the project

Activity 8. Revisit Activities 1-3 and Consider Performance Acceptance Criteria

Between iterations, ensure that the foundational information has not changed. Integrate new information, such as customer feedback, and update the strategy as necessary.

Checklist

Questions to ask:

- Have the performance implications of the project vision changed?
- Have the performance implications of the service we are trying to provide changed, or has the problem we are trying to solve for the customer changed?
- Have the project schedule, structure, or available resources changed?
- Have the performance-testing objectives changed?
- Have the performance-testing activities needed to validate any contractual, compliance, project, or customer performance criteria or expectations changed?
- What performance-testing activities will help address currently known performance concerns?

Value provided:

- Update resource and instrumentation assumptions and needs.
- Point out any areas of concern.
- Point out resource and instrumentation needs and/or risks.
- Update performance-testing objectives.
- Enhance and update usage scenarios of particular performance concerns.
- Enhance and update performance goals, requirements, targets, and thresholds.
- Ensure that the team has adequate warning about upcoming performance-testing activities that will require the support of additional team members.

Tasks accomplished:

- Enhance and update understanding of the project's critical performance implications.
- Update resource constraints; for example, budget, people, and equipment.
- Update/improve how the team will coordinate.
- Update/improve how the team will communicate.
- Revise performance-testing strategy.
- Refine estimates of equipment and/or resources required for conducting performance testing.
- Identify incompatibilities or conflicts between the objectives of the performance-testing effort and the equipment and resources to be made available.
- Capture additional performance goals, requirements, targets, and thresholds.
- Capture additional usage scenarios of particular concern.
- Report current performance-testing status.

Coordinate with:

- Whole team

Activity 9. Reprioritize Tasks

Based on the test results, new information, and the availability of features and components, reprioritize, add to, or delete tasks from the strategy, and then return to activity 5.

Checklist

Questions to ask:

- What performance-testing activities will help address currently known performance concerns?
- What is the performance goal for this cycle?
- Where is the project in terms of the overall project performance goals?
- Has the system achieved all of its performance objectives?
- Has tuning been accomplished since the last iteration?
- What analysis, reports, or retesting will add value during this iteration cycle?
- Who requires pairing to do performance testing?
- How much time is available?
- How much time does each task take?
- What is the most critical activity?

Value provided:

- Provide insight on how the overall project is achieving its goal.
- Provide insight on what can be measured and reported on in this cycle.
- Provide insight on any critical issues that may have arisen from the last iteration.
- Make suggestions to other team members.
- Transfer lessons learned as they emerge from the test.
- Pair with developers to improve performance unit testing.
- Help reuse unit tests.
- Help reuse functional tests.

Tasks accomplished:

- Report current performance-testing status.
- Estimate how much work is achievable.
- Determine if anyone needs to be paired out.
- Prioritize achievable work.
- Identify primary and alternate tasks for this cycle.

Coordinate with:

- Managers and stakeholders
- Developers and administrators
- Infrastructure and test environment support
- Users or user representatives

Summary

Performance testing with iteration-based processes is a common practice in development cycles such as Agile, XP, RUP, and other sources. To be effective, performance testing should be managed correctly in the context of iteration planning and processes.

6

Managing an Agile Performance Test Cycle

Objectives

- Learn an approach to agile performance test management.
- Learn how to maximize flexibility without sacrificing control.
- Learn how to provide managers and stakeholders with progress and value indicators.
- Learn how to provide a structure for capturing information that will not noticeably impact the release schedule.
- Learn how to apply an approach designed to embrace change, not simply tolerate it.

Overview

This chapter describes an agile approach to managing application performance testing. As the term implies, the key to an agile approach is flexibility. Flexibility, however, does not mean sloppiness or inefficiency. To remain efficient and thorough in an agile environment, you may need to change the way you are used to managing your performance testing.

Implementing an agile philosophy means different things to different teams, ranging from perfectly implemented eXtreme Programming (XP) to projects with many short iterations and documentation designed for efficiency. The approach outlined in this chapter has been successfully applied by teams across this spectrum with minimal modification.

This chapter assumes that the performance specialist is new to the team in question and focuses on the tasks that the performance specialist frequently drives or champions. This is neither an attempt to minimize the concept of team responsibility nor an attempt to segregate roles. The team is best served if the performance specialist is an integral team member who participates in team practices, such as pairing. Any sense of segregation is unintentional and a result of trying to simplify explanations.

This approach to managing performance testing may seem complicated at first because it:

- Embraces change during a project's life cycle.
- Iterates (not always in a predictable pattern).
- Encourages planning just far enough in advance for team coordination but not so far that the plan is likely to need significant revision in order to execute.

However, when viewed at the task or work item level, this approach is actually an intuitive process based on the principle of continually asking and answering the question, "What task can I do right now that will add the most value to the project?"

How to Use This Chapter

Use this chapter to understand the approach to performance testing in agile development environments and its relationship with the core activities of performance testing. Also use the chapter to understand what is accomplished during these activities. To get the most from this chapter:

- Use the "Agile Performance Testing Activities" section to get an overview of the approach to performance testing in agile environments, and as quick reference guide for you and your team.
- Use the various activity sections to understand the details of the most critical performance-testing tasks.
- Additionally, use Chapter 4, "Core Activities" in this guide to understand the common core activities involved in successful performance testing projects. This will help you to apply the concepts underlying those activities to a particular approach to performance testing.

Introduction to the Approach

When viewed from a linear perspective, the approach starts by examining the software development project as a whole, the reasons why stakeholders have chosen to include performance testing in the project, and the value that performance testing is expected to add to the project. The results of this examination include the team's view of the success criteria for the performance testing effort.

Once the success criteria are understood at a high level, an overall strategy is envisioned to guide the general approach to achieving those criteria by summarizing what performance testing activities are anticipated to add the most value at various points during the development life cycle. Those points may include key project deliveries, checkpoints, sprints, iterations, or weekly builds. For the purposes of this chapter, these events are collectively referred to as "performance builds". Frequently, while the strategy is evolving, the performance specialist and/or the team will begin setting up a performance-test environment and a load-generation environment.

With a strategy in mind and the necessary environments in place, the test team draws up plans for major tests or tasks identified for imminent performance builds. When a performance build is delivered, the plan's tasks should be executed in priority sequence (based on all currently available information), appropriately reporting, recording, revising, reprioritizing, adding, and removing tasks and improving the application and the overall plan as the work progresses.

Agile Performance-Testing Activities

This approach can be represented by using the following nine activities:

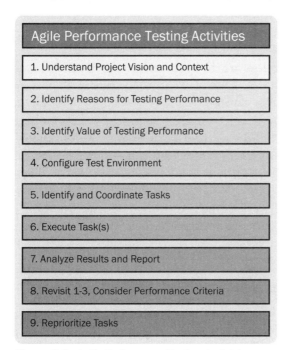

Figure 6.1 *Agile Performance Testing Activities*

- **Activity 1. Understand the Project Vision and Context.** The project vision and context are the foundation for determining what performance-testing activities are necessary and valuable.

- **Activity 2. Identify Reasons for Testing Performance.** These are not always clear from the vision and context. Explicitly identifying the reasons for performance testing is critical to being able to determine what performance testing activities will add the most value to the project.

- **Activity 3. Identify the Value Performance Testing Adds to the Project.** With the information gained from steps 1 and 2, clarify the value added through performance testing and convert that value into a conceptual performance-testing strategy.

- **Activity 4. Configure the Test Environment**. With a conceptual strategy in place, prepare the necessary tools and resources to execute the strategy as features and components become available for test.

- **Activity 5. Identify and Coordinate Immediately Valuable Tactical Tasks.** Performance-testing tasks do not happen in isolation. For this reason, the performance specialist needs to work with the team to prioritize and coordinate support, resources, and schedules in order to make the tasks efficient and successful.

- **Activity 6. Execute Task(s).** Conduct tasks in one- to two-day segments. See them through to completion, but be willing to take important detours along the way if an opportunity to add additional value presents itself.

- **Activity 7. Analyze Results and Report.** To keep up with an iterative process, results need to be analyzed and shared quickly. If the analysis is inconclusive, retest at the earliest possible opportunity. This gives the team the most time to react to performance issues.

- **Activity 8. Revisit Activities 1-3 and Consider Performance Acceptance Criteria.** Between iterations, ensure that the foundational information has not changed. Integrate new information such as customer feedback and update the strategy as necessary

- **Activity 9. Reprioritize Tasks.** Based on the test results, new information, and the availability of features and components, reprioritize, add to, or delete tasks from the strategy, then return to activity 5.

Relationship to Core Performance-Testing Activities

The following graphic shows how the seven core activities described in Chapter 4 map to the nine agile performance-testing activities.

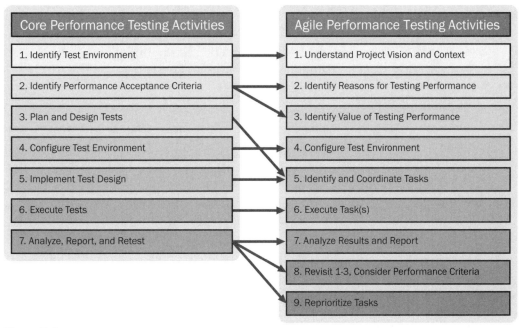

Figure 6.2 *Relationship to Core Performance Testing Activities*

Activity 1. Understand the Project Vision and Context

The project vision and context are the foundation for determining what performance testing is necessary and valuable. The test team's initial understanding of the system under test, the project environment, the motivation behind the project, and the performance build schedule can often be completed during a work session involving the performance specialist, the lead developer, and the project manager (if you also have a tentative project schedule). Decisions made during the work session can be refactored during other iteration and work sessions as the system becomes more familiar.

Project Vision

Before initiating performance testing, ensure that you understand the current project vision. Because the features, implementation, architecture, timeline, and environments are likely to change over time, you should revisit the vision regularly, as it has the potential to change as well. Although every team member should be thinking about performance, it is the performance specialist's responsibility to be proactive in understanding and keeping up to date with the relevant details across the entire team. The following are examples of high-level project visions:

- Evaluate a new architecture for an existing system.
- Develop a new custom system to solve a specific business problem.

- Evaluate the new software-development tools.
- As a team, become proficient in a new language or technology.
- Re-engineer an inadequate application before a period of peak user activity to avoid user dissatisfaction due to application failure.

Project Context

The project context is nothing more than those factors that are, or may become, relevant to achieving the project vision. Some examples of items that may be relevant to your project context include:

- Client expectations
- Budget
- Timeline
- Staffing
- Project environment
- Management approach

These items will often be discussed during a project kickoff meeting but, again, should be revisited regularly throughout the project as more details become available and as the team learns more about the system they are developing.

Understand the System

Understanding the system you are testing involves becoming familiar with the system's intent, what is currently known or assumed about its hardware and software architecture, and the available information about the completed system's customer or user.

With many agile projects, the system's architecture and functionality change over the course of the project. Expect this. In fact, the performance testing you do is frequently the driver behind at least some of those changes. Keeping this in mind will help you ensure that performance-testing tasks are neither over-planned nor under-planned before testing begins.

Understand the Project Environment

In terms of the project environment, it is most important to understand the team's organization, operation, and communications techniques. Agile teams tend not to use long-lasting documents and briefings as their management and communications methods; instead, they opt for daily stand-ups, story cards, and interactive discussions. Failing to understand these methods at the beginning of a project can put performance testing behind before it even begins. Asking the following or similar questions may be helpful:

- Does the team have any scheduled meetings, stand-ups, or scrums?
- How are issues raised or results reported?

- If I need to collaborate with someone, should I send an e-mail message? Schedule a meeting? Use Instant Messenger? Walk over to his or her office?

- Does this team employ a "do not disturb" protocol when an individual or sub-team desires "quiet time" to complete a particularly challenging task?

- Who is authorized to update the project plan or project board?

- How are tasks assigned and tracked? Software system? Story cards? Sign-ups?

- How do I determine which builds I should focus on for performance testing? Daily builds? Friday builds? Builds with a special tag?

- How do performance testing builds get promoted to the performance test environment?

- Will the developers be writing performance unit tests? Can I pair with them periodically so that we can share information?

- How do you envision coordination of performance-testing tasks?

Understand the Performance Build Schedule

At this stage, the project schedule makes its entrance, and it does not matter whether the project schedule takes the form of a desktop calendar, story cards, whiteboards, a document, someone's memory, or a software-based project management system. However, someone or something must communicate the anticipated sequence of deliveries, features, and/or hardware implementations that relate to the performance success criteria.

Because you are not creating a performance test plan at this time, remember that it is not important to concern yourself with dates or resources. Instead, attend to the anticipated sequencing of performance builds, a rough estimate of their contents, and an estimate of how much time to expect between performance builds. The specific performance builds that will most likely interest you relate to hardware components, supporting software, and application functionality becoming available for investigation.

Typically, you will find during this step that you add performance build–specific items to your success criteria, and that you start aligning tasks related to achieving success criteria with anticipated performance builds.

Activity 2. Identify Reasons for Testing Performance

The underlying reasons for testing performance on a particular project are not always obvious based on just the vision and context. Explicitly identifying the reasons for performance testing is critical to being able to determine what performance-testing activities will add the most value to the project.

The reasons for conducting performance testing often go beyond a list of performance acceptance criteria. Every project has different reasons for deciding to include, or not include, performance testing as part of its process. Not identifying and understanding these reasons is one way to virtually guarantee that the performance-testing aspect of the project will not be as successful as it could have been. Examples of possible reasons to make integrated performance testing a part of the project include the following:

- Improve performance unit testing by pairing performance testers with developers.
- Assess and configure new hardware by pairing performance testers with administrators.
- Evaluate algorithm efficiency.
- Monitor resource usage trends.
- Measure response times.
- Collect data for scalability and capacity planning.

It is generally useful to identify the reasons for conducting performance testing very early in the project. Because these reasons are bound to change and/or shift priority as the project progresses, you should revisit them regularly as you and your team learn more about the application, its performance, and the customer or user.

Success Criteria

It is also useful to start identifying the desired success criteria associated with the reasons for conducting performance testing, early in the project. As with the reasons for testing, the success criteria are bound to change, so you should revisit them regularly as you and your team learn more about the application, its performance, and the customer or user. Success criteria not only include the performance requirements, goals, and targets for the application, but also the objectives behind conducting performance testing in the first place, including those objectives that are financial or educational in nature. For example, success criteria may include:

- Validate that the application be able to handle X users per hour.
- Validate that the users will experience response times of Y seconds or less 95 percent of the time.
- Validate that performance tests predict production performance within a +/- 10-percent range of variance.
- Investigate hardware and software as it becomes available, to detect significant performance issues early.
- The performance team, developers, and administrators work together with minimal supervision to tune and determine the capacity of the architecture.
- Conduct performance testing within the existing project duration and budget.

- Determine the most likely failure modes for the application under higher-than-expected load conditions.
- Determine appropriate system configuration settings for desired performance characteristics.

It is important to record the performance success criteria in a manner appropriate to your project's standards and expectations, in a location where they are readily accessible to the entire team. Whether the criteria appear in the form of a document, on story cards, on a team wiki, in a task-management system, or on a whiteboard is important only to the degree that it works for your team.

The initial determination of performance-testing success criteria can often be accomplished in a single work session involving the performance specialist, the lead developer, and the project manager. Because you are articulating and recording success criteria for the performance-testing effort, and not creating a performance-test plan, it is not important to concern yourself with dates and resources.

In general, consider the following information when determining performance-testing success criteria:

- Application performance requirements and goals
- Performance-related targets and thresholds
- Exit criteria (how to know when you are done)
- Key areas of investigation
- Key data to be collected

Activity 3. Identify the Value Performance Testing Adds to the Project

Using the information gained in activities 1 and 2, clarify the value added through performance testing and convert that value into a conceptual performance-testing strategy.

Now that you have an up-to-date understanding of the system, the project, and the performance testing success criteria, you can begin conceptualizing an overall strategy for performance-testing imminent performance builds. It is important to communicate the strategy to the entire team, using a method that encourages feedback and discussion.

Strategies should not contain excessive detail or narrative text. These strategies are intended to help focus decisions, be readily available to the entire team, include a method for anyone to make notes or comments, and be easy to modify as the project progresses.

While there is a wide range of information that could be included in the strategy, the critical components are the desired outcomes of the performance testing of the performance build and anticipated tasks that achieve that outcome. Although it seldom occurs, if you need significant resource coordination to accomplish a task, it might make sense to complete strategies a few performance builds in advance. Strategies are most often completed roughly concurrent with the release of a performance build.

Discussion Points

In general, the types of information that may be valuable to discuss with the team when preparing a performance-testing strategy for a performance build include:

- The reason for performance testing this delivery
- Prerequisites for strategy execution
- Tools and scripts required
- External resources required
- Risks to accomplishing the strategy
- Data of special interest
- Areas of concern
- Pass/fail criteria
- Completion criteria
- Planned variants on tests
- Load range
- Tasks to accomplish the strategy

Activity 4. Configure the Test Environment

With a conceptual strategy in place, prepare the necessary tools and resources to execute the strategy as features and components become available for test.

Load-generation and application-monitoring tools are almost never as easy to implement as one expects. Whether issues arise from setting up isolated network environments, procuring hardware, coordinating a dedicated bank of IP addresses for IP spoofing, or version compatibility between monitoring software and server operating systems, issues always seem to arise.

Also, it is inevitable that load-generation tools always lag behind evolving technologies and practices. Tool creators can only build in support for the most prominent technologies, and even then, the technologies have to become prominent before the support can be built.

This often means that the biggest challenge involved in a performance-testing project is getting your first relatively realistic test implemented with users generally being simulated in such a way that the application under test cannot legitimately tell the difference between simulated and real users. Plan for this and do not be surprised when it takes significantly longer than expected to get it all working smoothly.

Additionally, plan to periodically reconfigure, update, add to, or otherwise enhance your load-generation environment and associated tools throughout the project. Even if the application under test stays the same and the load-generation tool is working properly, it is likely that the metrics you want to collect will change. This frequently implies some degree of change to or addition of monitoring tools.

Activity 5. Identify and Coordinate Tasks

Performance-testing tasks do not happen in isolation. The performance specialist needs to work with the team to prioritize and coordinate support, resources, and schedules to make the tasks efficient and successful.

As a delivery approaches, you will want to create performance test execution plans for each one to two days' worth of performance-testing tasks. This means you are likely to have several performance test execution plans per performance build. Each of these execution plans should communicate the remaining details needed to complete or repeat a work item or group of work items.

Performance test execution plans should be communicated to the team and stakeholders by using the same method(s) the strategy uses. Depending on the pace and schedule of your project, there may be one execution plan per strategy, or several. It is important to limit the execution plans to one or two days of anticipated tasks for several reasons, including the following:

- Even though each task or group of tasks is planned to take one or two days, it is not uncommon for the actual execution to stretch to three or even four days on occasion. If your plans are for tasks longer than about two days and you get delayed, you are likely to have the next performance build before completing any valuable testing on the previous build.

- Especially on agile projects, timely feedback about performance is critical. Even with two-day tasks and a one-week performance build cycle, you could end up with approximately eight days between detecting an issue and getting a performance build that addresses that issue. With longer tasks and/or a longer period between performance builds, those 8 days can quickly become 16.

Performance test execution plans should be communicated far enough in advance to be shared with the team—for recommendations or improvements, and for necessary resource coordination to take place—but nothing further. Due to the specificity of the execution plan, preparing them well in advance almost always leads to significant rework. In most cases, the team as a whole will prioritize the sequence of execution of tasks.

Discussion Points

In general, the types of information that a team finds valuable when discussing a performance test execution plan for a work item or group of work items include:

- Work item execution method
- Specifically what data will be collected
- Specifically how that data will be collected
- Who will assist, how, and when
- Sequence of work items by priority

Activity 6. Execute Task(s)

Conduct tasks in one-to-two day segments. See them through to completion, but be willing to take important detours along the way if an opportunity to add additional value presents itself.

When each performance build is delivered, the performance testing begins with the highest-priority task related to that build. Early in the development life cycle, those tasks are likely to contain work items such as "collaborate with administrators to tune application servers," while later in the development cycle, a work item might be "validate that the application is achieving response time goals at 50 percent of peak load."

The most important part of task execution is to remember to modify the task and subsequent strategies as results analysis leads to new priorities. After a task is executed, share your findings with the team, and then reprioritize the remaining tasks, add new tasks, and/or remove planned tasks from execution plans and strategies based on the new questions and concerns raised by the team. When reprioritizing is complete, move on to the next-highest-priority task.

Keys to Conducting a Performance-Testing Task

In general, the keys to conducting a performance-testing task include:

- Analyze results immediately and revise the plan accordingly.
- Work closely with the team or sub-team that is most relevant to the task.
- Communicate frequently and openly across the team.
- Record results and significant findings.
- Record other data needed to repeat the test later.
- Revisit performance-testing priorities after no more than two days.

Activity 7. Analyze Results and Report

To keep up with an iterative process, results need to be analyzed and shared quickly. If the analysis is inconclusive, retest at the earliest possible opportunity. This gives the team the most time to react to performance issues.

Even though you are sharing data and preliminary results at the completion of each task, it is important to pause periodically to consolidate results, conduct trend analysis, create stakeholder reports, and pair with developers, architects, and administrators to analyze results. Periodically may mean a half-day per week, one day between performance builds, or some other interval that fits smoothly into your project workflow.

These short pauses are often where the "big breaks" occur. Although continual reporting keeps the team informed, these reports are generally summaries delivered as an e-mailed paragraph with a spreadsheet attached, or a link to the most interesting graph on the project Web site.

On their own, these reports rarely tell the whole story. One of the jobs of the performance specialist is to find trends and patterns in the data, which takes time. This task also tends to lead to the desire to re-execute one or more tests to determine if a pattern really exists, or if a particular test was flawed in some way. Teams are often tempted to skip this step, but do not yield to that temptation. You might end up with more data more quickly, but if you do not stop to look at the data collectively on a regular basis, you are unlikely to extract all of the useful findings from that data until it is too late.

Activity 8. Revisit Activities 1-3 and Consider Performance Acceptance Criteria

Between iterations, ensure that the foundational information has not changed. Integrate new information such as customer feedback and update the strategy as necessary.

After the success criteria, strategies, and/or tasks have been updated and prioritized, it is time to resume the performance-testing process where you left off. However, this is easier said than done. Sometimes, no matter how hard you try to avoid it, there are simply no valuable performance-testing tasks to conduct at this point. This could be due to environment upgrades, mass re-architecting/refactoring, significant detected performance issues that someone else needs time to fix, and so on.

On the positive side, the performance specialist has possibly the broadest set of skills on the entire team. This means that when the situation arises, continued performance testing or paired performance investigation with developers or administrators is not going to add value at this time, and the performance specialist can be temporarily given another task such as automating smoke tests, optimizing HTML for better performance, pairing with a developer to assist with developing more comprehensive unit tests, and so on. The key is to never forget that the performance specialist's first priority is performance testing, while these other tasks are additional responsibilities.

Activity 9. Reprioritize Tasks

Based on the test results, new information, and the availability of features and components, reprioritize, add to, or delete tasks from the strategy, and then return to activity 5.

Some agile teams conduct periodic "performance-only" scrums or stand-ups when performance testing–related coordination, reporting, or analysis is too time-consuming to be handled in the existing update structure. Whether during a special "performance-only" scrum or stand-up or during existing sessions, the team collectively makes most of the major adjustments to priorities, strategies, tasks, and success criteria. Ensure that enough time is allocated frequently enough for the team to make good performance-related decisions, while changes are still easy to make.

The key to successfully implementing an agile performance-testing approach is continual communication among team members. As described in the previous steps, it is a good idea not only to communicate tasks and strategies with all team members, checking back with one another frequently, but also to plan time into testing schedules to review and update tasks and priorities.

The methods you use to communicate plans, strategies, priorities, and changes are completely irrelevant as long as you are able to adapt to changes without requiring significant rework, and as long as the team continues to progress toward achieving the current performance-testing success criteria.

Additional Considerations

Keep in mind the following additional considerations for managing an agile performance test cycle:

- The best advice is to remember to communicate all significant information and findings to the team.

- No matter how long or short the time between performance builds, performance testing will always lag behind. Too many performance-testing tasks take too long to develop and execute to keep up with development in real time. Keep this in mind when setting priorities for what to performance-test next. Choose wisely.

- Remember that for the vast majority of the development life cycle, performance testing is about collecting useful information to enhance performance through design, architecture, and development as it happens. Comparisons against the end user–focused requirements and goals only have meaning for customer review releases or production release candidates. The rest of the time, you are looking for trends and obvious problems, not pass/fail validation.

- Make use of existing unit-testing code for performance testing at the component level. Doing so is quick, easy; helps the developers detect trends in performance, and can make a powerful smoke test.
- Do not force a performance build just because it is on the schedule. If the current build is not appropriate for performance testing, continue with what you have until it is appropriate, or give the performance tester another task until something reasonable is ready.
- Performance testing is one of the single biggest catalysts to significant changes in architecture, code, hardware, and environments. Use this to your advantage by making observed performance issues highly visible across the entire team. Simply reporting on performance every day or two is not enough—the team needs to read, understand, and react to the reports, or else the performance testing loses much of its value.

Summary

Performance testing in an agile project environment allows you to manage the testing in a highly flexible way. In particular, this approach allows you to revisit the project vision and reprioritize tasks based on the value they add to the performance test at a given point in time.

7

Managing the Performance Test Cycle in a Regulated (CMMI) Environment

Objectives

- Become familiar with a performance test management approach appropriate for CMMI, auditable, and highly regulated projects.
- Learn how to maximize effectiveness without sacrificing control or compliance.
- Learn how to provide managers and stakeholders with progress and value indicators.
- Learn how to provide a structure for capturing information within the schedule, not in addition to it.
- Learn how to apply an approach designed to adapt to change without generating excessive rework, management, or audit concerns.

Overview

In today's software-engineering industry, the complexity and critical nature of some of the systems necessitates regulatory oversight. It is always a challenge to balance the pressure of oversight with staying flexible enough to engineer a system effectively and efficiently. There is no reason why regulatory compliance and flexibility cannot work well together — you need only expand the task list and accept some tradeoffs in the schedule and engineering resources.

Capability Maturity Model® Integration (CMMI) is used here as a paradigmatic example of a process generally viewed as anything but flexible. CMMI is frequently seen as a heavyweight approach, generally more appropriate for safety-critical software and software that is subject to regulatory standards and/or process audits. CMMI was created by the Software Engineering Institute at Carnegie Mellon University and is defined as follows:

> "Capability Maturity Model® Integration (CMMI) is a process improvement approach that provides organizations with the essential elements of effective processes. It can be used to guide process improvement across a project, a division, or an entire organization."

The nature of performance testing makes it difficult to predict what type of test will add value, or even be possible. Obviously, this makes planning all the more challenging. This chapter describes an industry-validated approach to planning and managing performance testing. This approach is sensitive to the need for auditability, progress tracking, and changes to plans that require approval without being oppressively procedural.

How to Use This Chapter

Use this chapter to understand the approach for performance testing in regulated (CMMI) development environments and its relationship with the core activities of performance testing. Also use this chapter to understand what is accomplished during these activities. To get the most from this chapter:

- Use the "CMMI Performance-Testing Activities" section to get an overview of the approach to performance testing in CMMI environments, and as quick reference guide for you and your team.

- Use the various activity sections to understand the details of the most critical performance-testing tasks.

- Additionally, use Chapter 4, "Core Activities" in this guide to understand the common core activities involved in successful performance-testing projects. This will help you to apply the concepts underlying those activities to a particular approach to performance testing.

Introduction to the Approach

The key to the approach is to plan at the performance test work item level and to fit those work items into the existing plan for accomplishing the project. This allows for compliance, auditability, and approval gates while leaving the execution details in the hands of those assigned to complete a particular work item.

When viewed from a linear perspective, the approach starts by examining the software-development project as a whole, the relevant processes and standards, and the performance acceptance criteria for the system. The results of this examination include the team's view of the success criteria for the performance-testing effort.

Once the success and acceptance criteria are understood at a high level, planning and test design become the primary activities. The resulting plan and test design should guide the general approach to achieving those criteria by summarizing what performance testing activities are anticipated to add the most value at various points during the development cycle. These points may include key project deliveries, checkpoints, iterations, or weekly builds. For the purposes of this chapter, these events are collectively referred to as "performance builds". Frequently, while the plan and test design is evolving, the performance specialist and/or the team will begin setting up a performance test environment including the system under test and a load-generation environment that includes monitoring and load-generation tools.

With a plan, test design, and the necessary environments in place, test designs are implemented for major tests, or work items are identified for imminent performance builds. When performance-testing for a particular performance build is complete, it is time to report, archive data, and update the performance test plan and test designs as appropriate, ensuring that the correct processes are followed and approvals obtained. Ultimately, the final performance build will be tested and it will be time to compile the final report.

CMMI Performance-Testing Activities

This approach described in this chapter can be represented by the following 12 activities.

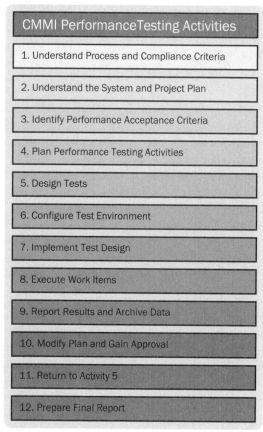

CMMI PerformanceTesting Activities

1. Understand Process and Compliance Criteria
2. Understand the System and Project Plan
3. Identify Performance Acceptance Criteria
4. Plan Performance Testing Activities
5. Design Tests
6. Configure Test Environment
7. Implement Test Design
8. Execute Work Items
9. Report Results and Archive Data
10. Modify Plan and Gain Approval
11. Return to Activity 5
12. Prepare Final Report

Figure 7.1 *CMMI Performance Testing Activities*

- **Activity 1. Understand the Process and Compliance Criteria.** This activity involves building an understanding of the process and the compliance requirements.

- **Activity 2. Understand the System and the Project Plan.** Establish a fairly detailed understanding of the system you are to test and the project specifics for the development of that system.

- **Activity 3. Identify Performance Acceptance Criteria.** This activity includes identifying the performance goals and requirements. This also includes identifying the performance testing objectives.

- **Activity 4. Plan Performance-Testing Activities.** This activity includes mapping work items to the project plan, determining durations, prioritizing the work, and adding detail to the plan.

- **Activity 5. Design Tests.** This activity involves identifying key usage scenarios, determining appropriate user variances, identifying and generating test data, and specifying the metrics to be collected.

- **Activity 6. Configure the Test Environment.** This activity involves setting up your actual test environment.

- **Activity 7. Implement the Test Design.** This activity involves creating your tests.

- **Activity 8. Execute Work Items.** This activity involves executing your performance test work items.

- **Activity 9. Report Results and Archive Data.** This activity involves consolidating results and sharing data among the team.

- **Activity 10. Modify the Plan and Gain Approval for Modifications.** This activity involves reviewing and adjusting the plan as needed.

- **Activity 11. Return to Activity 5.** This activity involves continuous testing through the next delivery, iteration, and checkpoint release.

- **Activity 12. Prepare the Final Report.** This activity involves the creation, submission, and acceptance of the final report.

Relationship to Core Performance-Testing Activities

The following graphic show how the seven core activities from Chapter 4 map to these twelve activities:

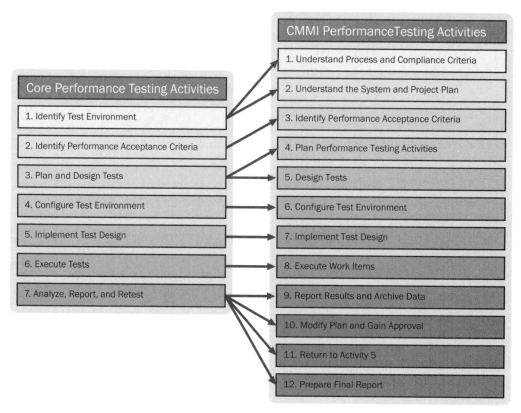

Figure 7.2 *Relationship to Core Performance Testing Activities*

CMMI Performance Testing Activity Flow

The following graphic is more representative of an actual instance of this performance-testing approach. The graphic shows that there is a more or less well-defined, linear structure that has clear places for approval gates, re-planning, and checkpoints. The loop from activity 11 back to activity 5 illustrates how the same basic approach is followed iteration after iteration.

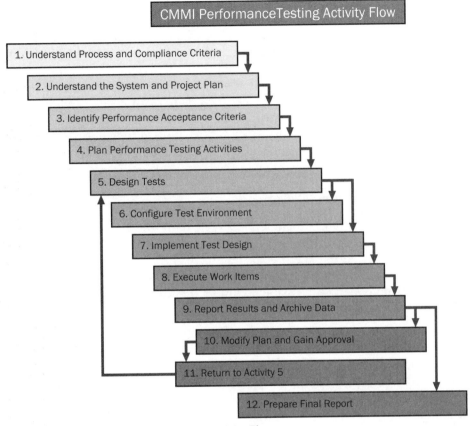

Figure 7.3 *CMMI Performance Testing Activity Flow*

Activity 1. Understand the Process and Compliance Criteria

This step has almost nothing to do with performance testing, yet it is absolutely critical to the overall success of the performance testing sub-project. Performance testing can be complex enough, even without finding out in the middle of the process that you need to reproduce test data or results from previously conducted tests because an audit is scheduled to take place in two weeks.

You must completely understand the process and compliance requirements even before you start planning your performance testing, because it is the only way to ensure that the testing effort does not get derailed or stuck in a bureaucratic process of change-request approvals and sign-offs. Fortunately, these rules and regulations are almost always thoroughly documented, making this step relatively straightforward, and the challenges frequently lie in obtaining and interpreting these documents.

Determine the Process

Process documentation is typically easy to obtain   the challenge lies in understanding and interpreting how that process applies to performance testing. Software development process documentation rarely addresses performance testing directly. If this is the case for your project, perhaps the best way to determine the appropriate process is to extrapolate the document to include performance testing to the extent possible, and then submit the revised process to the project manager and/or process engineer for approval. You may have to iterate before getting approval, but it is still better to submit the performance-testing process concept before the project launches than afterward.

Determine Compliance Criteria

Regulatory and compliance documents may be harder to obtain because they often are not made readily available for review by non-executives. Even so, it is important to review these standards. The specific language and context of any statement related to testing is critical to determining a compliant process. The nature of performance testing makes it virtually impossible to follow the same processes that have been developed for functional testing.

For example, when executing a performance test simulating hundreds of users, if three of those users record response times that do not achieve the documented requirement, does that requirement pass or fail? Which test case does that count against, the one that sets the response time, the volume, or the workload? Does the entire test fail? What happens to the thousands of other measurements collected during the test? Do those three failing measurements get one defect report, or three, or none, because the average response time was acceptable? These are the kinds of questions you will likely face and need to resolve based on whatever specific standards have been applied to your project.

Once you understand both the process and the compliance criteria, take the time to get your interpretations approved by an appropriate stakeholder. Compliance is not your specialty; performance testing is. Get help when you need it.

Activity 2. Understand the System and the Project Plan

Once you have a firm understanding of the process and compliance requirements, the next step is to establish a fairly detailed understanding of the system you are to test and the project specifics for the development of that system. Again, in a CMMI-type project, there are usually many documents to read and project plans to reference. These may include use case documents and models, state-transition diagrams, logical and physical architecture diagrams, storyboards, prototypes, contracts, and requirements. Although all of these documents are valuable, even when taken together, they frequently do not contain all of the information you will need in order to create an adequate performance test plan.

Understand the System

The information about the system contained in these documents is frequently abstracted from the end user in such a way that it is difficult to envision how individuals and groups of users will interact with the system. This is where you need to put your business analyst skills to use. Some of the things you will want to make sure you understand include:

- Who or what are the users of the system? What are their reasons for using the system, their expectations, and their motivations?
- What are the most frequently occurring usage scenarios for the system?
- What are the business-critical usage scenarios for the system?
- What are the different ways that a user can accomplish a task with system?
- How frequently will a user access the system?
- What is the relative distribution of tasks that a group of users will conduct over time?
- How many users are likely to interact with the system at different points in time?

Review the Project Plan

With the system information in hand, it is time to turn to the project plan. It is important to remember that performance testing is a sub-project, not the main project. Therefore it is your responsibility to blend performance testing into the plan with as little overall impact to the project as possible. This is where milestones, checkpoints, builds, and iterations come in.

The specific items you are mostly likely to be interested in relate to hardware components, supporting software, and application functionality becoming available for performance testing. Coupling this information with the compliance criteria; requirements, goals, and objectives, as well as the information you have collected about the system and its usage, you can put together a performance test plan that fits into the project without adding unnecessary overhead.

Activity 3. Identify Performance Acceptance Criteria

Regardless of the process your team is following, it is a good idea to at least start identifying desired performance characteristics of an application early in the development life cycle. This is frequently more important to complete prior to starting your testing, when you have the added pressure of having to record, demonstrate, and possibly get approval for how you are going to validate each of these characteristics.

Performance Requirements

Remember that requirements are those characteristics required by contract, law, or a significant stakeholder. When facing roadblocks to reviewing contracts, it is important to explain that the specific language and context of any statement related to application performance is critical to determining compliance. For example, the difference between "transactions will" and "on average, transactions will" is tremendous. The first case implies that every transaction will comply every single time. The second case is completely ambiguous, as you will see in below.

To determine requirements, focus on contracts and legally binding agreements, or standards related to the software under development. Also, get the executive stakeholders to commit to any performance conditions that might cause them to refuse to release the software into production. The resulting criteria may or may not be related to any specific business transaction or condition, but if they are, you must ensure that those transactions or conditions are included in your performance testing.

Performance Goals

Performance goals can be more challenging to determine. Performance goals are those characteristics that are desired by stakeholders, users, developers, or other interested individuals, but that will not automatically prevent shipment of the product if the goals are not exactly met. Good sources for soliciting performance goals include:

- Project documentation and contracts
- Interviews with stakeholders
- Competitive analysis
- Usability studies

Performance-Testing Objectives

The performance tester does not always have easy access to either explicit or implied objectives, and therefore frequently must conduct a systematic search for them. The easiest way to determine and record performance-testing objectives is simply to ask each member of the project team what value you can add for him or her while you are performance testing at a particular point in the project, or immediately following the accomplishment of a particular milestone.

While it is not always easy to find and schedule time with each member of the team—especially when you consider that the project team includes executive stakeholders, analysts, and possibly even representative users—team members are generally receptive to sharing information that will help you establish valuable performance-testing objectives.

Such objectives might include providing resource utilization data under load, generating specific loads to assist with tuning an application server, or providing a report of the number of objects requested by each Web page. Although it is most valuable to collect performance-testing objectives early in the project life cycle, it is also important to periodically revisit these objectives, ask team members if they would like to see any new objectives added, and gain approval for changes or additions as necessary.

Once you have determined the performance requirements, goals, and testing objectives, record them in a manner appropriate to your process. This often includes a formal document and entry into a requirements-management system.

Activity 4. Plan Performance-Testing Activities

All test plans are challenging to do well. To have any realistic hope of creating a plan that will more or less guide the performance-testing activities for the duration of the project without needing a major overhaul, you need to both forward- and reverse-engineer the plan to accommodate what testing "must" be done, what testing "should" be done, and when any particular test "can" be done.

Map Work Items to Project Plan

You can accomplish this by mapping performance requirements, goals, and objectives, as well as compliance criteria, against the key deliveries, milestones, iterations, and checkpoints. The following table provides an example of this mapping.

	Iteration 1	Iteration 2	Iteration 3	Checkpoint 1
500 users will be able to log in over a 5-minute period (interim and final requirement).			X	✓
All page response times will be under 6 seconds (goal).	X	X	X	X
Tune application server for improved performance and scalability (objective).		X	X	X
Ensure that all procedures, scripts, data, and results from tests used to validate interim or final requirements are archived sufficiently to repeat the test and results later, if needed (compliance).				✓

In this table, an 'X' represents a compliance task or test case (generically referred to as work items) that can be accomplished during a particular test phase according to the project plan. A '✓' represents a work item that must be accomplished during a particular test phase because of performance or compliance requirements.

Add Durations

Next, add the duration of each phase and the estimated duration of each work item.

	Iteration 1 1 week	Iteration 2 1 week	Iteration 3 1 week	Checkpoint 1 2 weeks
500 users will be able to log in over a 5-minute period (interim and final requirement).			X (2 days)	✓ (2 days)
All page response times will be under 6 seconds (goal).	X (2 days)	X (2 days)	X (2 days)	X (2 days)
Tune application server for improved performance and scalability (objective).		X (3 days)	X (3 days)	X (3 days)
Ensure that all procedures, scripts, data, and results from tests used to validate interim or final requirements are archived sufficiently to repeat the test and results later, if needed (compliance).				✓ (3 days)

Prioritize Work Items by Phase

The previous section covered the forward-engineering aspect of planning performance-testing activities. Now that you have added this information, you apply reverse-engineering to determine which work items will be accomplished during which phase to ensure that all work items are appropriately covered. The following table provides an example.

	Iteration 1 1 week	Iteration 2 1 week	Iteration 3 1 week	Checkpoint 1 2 weeks
500 users will be able to log in over a 5-minute period (interim and final requirement).		X (2 days)	X (2 days) Planned	✓ (2 days) Planned
All page response times will be under 6 seconds (goal).	X (2 days) Planned	X (2 days) Planned	X (2 days)	X (2 days) Planned
Tune application server for improved performance and scalability (objective).		X (3 days) Planned	X (3 days) Planned	X (3 days) Planned
Ensure that all procedures, scripts, data, and results from tests used to validate interim or final requirements are archived sufficiently to repeat the test and results later, if needed (compliance).				✓ (3 days) Planned

Add Detail to the Plan

Finally, with this information you can detail the plan for each work item to include:

- The reason for this test at this time
- Priority for execution at this time
- Prerequisites for execution
- Tools and scripts required
- External resources required
- Risks to completing the work item
- Data of special interest
- Areas of concern
- Pass/fail criteria
- Completion criteria
- Planned variants on tests
- Load range
- Specifically what data will be collected
- Specifically how that data will be collected
- Who will assist, how, and when
- Additional information needed to repeat the work item later, if needed

Completing this information constitutes a draft or initial performance test plan. In most cases, this draft should be reviewed, potentially enhanced, and approved by the appropriate managers or stakeholders prior to executing the plan.

Activity 5. Design Tests

Designing performance tests involves identifying key usage scenarios, determining appropriate user variances, identifying and generating test data, and specifying the metrics to be collected. Ultimately these items will provide the foundation for workloads and workload profiles.

When designing and planning tests, the intent is to simulate real-world tests that can provide reliable data to help facilitate making informed business decisions. Real-world test designs will significantly increase the reliability and usefulness of results data.

Key usage scenarios for the application under test typically surface during the process of identifying the application's desired performance characteristics. If this is not the case for your test project, you will need to explicitly determine the usage scenarios that are the most valuable to script. Consider the following when identifying key usage scenarios, remembering to think about both human and system users, such as batch processes and external applications:

- Contractually obligated usage scenario(s)
- Usage scenarios implied or mandated by performance-testing goals and objectives.
- Most common usage scenario(s)
- Business-critical usage scenario(s)
- Performance-intensive usage scenario(s)
- Usage scenarios of technical concern
- Usage scenarios of stakeholder concern
- High-visibility usage scenarios

After the key usage scenarios have been identified, they will need to be elaborated into tests. This elaboration process typically involves the following activities:

- Determine navigation paths for key scenarios.
- Determine individual user data and variances.
- Determine relative distribution of scenarios.
- Identify target load levels.
- Identify metrics to be captured during test execution.

Determine Navigation Paths for Key Scenarios

Human beings are unpredictable, and Web sites commonly offer redundant functionality. Even with a relatively small number of users, it is almost certain that real users will not only use every path you think they will to complete a task, but they also will inevitably invent some that you had not planned. Each path a user takes to complete an activity will place a different load on the system. That difference may be trivial, or it may be enormous—there is no way to be certain until you test it. There are many methods to determine navigation paths, including:

- Identifying the user paths within your Web application that are expected to have significant performance impact and that accomplish one or more of the identified key scenarios.

- Reading design and/or usage manuals.

- Trying to accomplish the activities yourself.

- Observing others trying to accomplish the activity without instruction (other than would be given to a new user prior to his or her first use of the system).

- Analyzing empirical data from Web server logs captured during pre-production releases and usage studies.

Determine Individual User Data and Variances

During the early stages of development and testing, user data and variances are most often estimated based on expected usage and observation of users working with similar applications. These estimates are generally enhanced or revised when empirical data from Web server logs becomes available. Some of the more useful metrics that can be read or interpreted from Web server logs include:

- **Page views per period.** A *page view* is a page request that includes all dependent file requests (.jpg files, CSS files, etc). Page views can be tracked over hourly, daily, or weekly time periods to account for cyclical patterns or bursts of peak user activity on the Web site.

- **User sessions per period.** A *user session* is the sequence of related requests originating from a user visit to the Web site, as explained previously. As with page views, user sessions can span hourly, daily, and weekly time periods.

- **Session duration.** This metric represents the amount of time a user session lasts, measured from the first page request until the last page request is completed, and including the time the user pauses for when navigating from page to page.

- **Page request distribution.** This metric represents the distribution, in percentages, of page hits according to functional types (Home, login, Pay, etc.). The distribution percentages will establish a weighting ratio of page hits based on the actual user utilization of the Web site.

- **Interaction speed.** Also known as "user think time," "page view time," and "user delay," this metric represents the time users take to transition between pages when navigating the Web site, constituting the think time behavior. It is important to remember that every user will interact with the Web site at a different rate.

- **User abandonment.** This metric represents the length of time that users will wait for a page to load before growing dissatisfied, exiting the site, and thus abandoning their user session. Abandoned sessions are quite normal on the Internet and consequently will have an impact on the load test results.

Determine the Relative Distribution of Scenarios

Having determined which scenarios to simulate and what the steps and associated data are for those scenarios, and having consolidated those scenarios into one or more workload models, you now need to determine how often users perform each activity represented in the model relative to the other activities needed to complete the workload model.

Sometimes one workload distribution is not enough. Research and experience have shown that user activities often vary greatly over time. To ensure test validity, you must validate that activities are evaluated according to time of day, day of week, day of month, and time of year. The most common methods for determining the relative distribution of activities include:

- Extract the actual usage, load values, common and uncommon usage scenarios (user paths), user delay time between clicks or pages, and input data variance (to name a few) directly from log files.

- Interview the individuals responsible for selling/marketing new features to find out what features/functions are expected and therefore most likely to be used. By interviewing existing users, you may also determine which of the new features/ functions they believe they are most likely to use.

- Deploy a beta release to a group of representative users—roughly 10-20 percent the size of the expected user base—and analyze the log files from their usage of the site.

- Run simple in-house experiments using employees, customers, clients, friends, or family members to determine, for example, natural user paths and the page-viewing time differences between new and returning users.

- As a last resort, you can use your intuition, or best guess, to make estimations based on your own familiarity with the site.

Once you are confident that the model is good enough for performance testing, supplement the model with the individual usage data you collected previously in such a way that the model contains all the data you need to create the actual test.

Identify Target Load Levels

A customer visit to a Web site comprises a series of related requests known as a user session. Users with different behaviors who navigate the same Web site are unlikely to cause overlapping requests to the Web server during their sessions. Therefore, instead of modeling the user experience on the basis of concurrent users, it is more useful to base your model on user sessions. User sessions can be defined as a sequence of actions in a navigational page flow, undertaken by a customer visiting a Web site.

Without some degree of empirical data, target load levels are exactly that—targets. These targets are most frequently set by the business, based on its goals related to the application and whether those goals are market penetration, revenue generation, or something else. These represent the numbers you want to work with at the outset.

As soon as Web server logs for a pre-production release or a current implementation of the application become available, you can use data from these logs to validate and/or enhance the data collected by using the resources above. By performing a quantitative analysis on Web server logs, you can determine:

- The total number of visits to the site over a period of time (month/week/day).
- The volume of usage, in terms of total averages and peak loads, on an hourly basis.
- The duration of sessions for total averages and peak loads, on an hourly basis.
- The total hourly averages and peak loads translated into overlapping user sessions to simulate real scalability volume for the load test.

By combining the volume information with objectives, key scenarios, user delays, navigation paths, and scenario distributions from the previous steps, you can determine the remaining details necessary to implement the workload model under a particular target load.

Identify Metrics to Be Captured During Test Execution

When identified, captured, and reported correctly, metrics provide information about how your application's performance compares to your desired performance characteristics. In addition, metrics can help you identify problem areas and bottlenecks within your application.

It is useful to identify the metrics that relate to the performance acceptance criteria during test design so that the method of collecting those metrics can be integrated into the tests when implementing the test design. When identifying metrics, use either specific desired characteristics or indicators that are directly or indirectly related to those characteristics.

Considerations

Consider the following key points when designing a test:

- Real-world test designs are sensitive to dependencies outside the control of the system, such as humans and other systems interacting with the application.
- Realistic test designs are based on real operations and data, not mechanistic procedures.
- Realistic test designs produce more credible results and thus enhance the value of performance testing.
- Realistic simulation of user delays and think times is crucial to the accuracy of the test.
- If users are likely to abandon a task for any reason, this should be accounted for in your test design.
- Remember to include common user errors in your scenarios.
- Component-level performance tests are an integral part of real-world testing.
- Real-world test designs can be more costly and time-consuming to implement, but they deliver far more accurate results to the business and stakeholders.
- Extrapolation of performance results from unrealistic tests can be inaccurate as the system scope increases, and frequently lead to poor decisions.
- Involve the developers and administrators in the process of determining which metrics are likely to add value and which method best integrates the capturing of those metrics into the test.
- Beware of allowing your tools to influence your test design. Better tests almost always result from designing tests on the assumption that they can be executed and then adapting the test or the tool when that assumption is proven false, rather than by *not* designing particular tests based on the assumption that you do not have access to a tool to execute the test.

Activity 6. Configure the Test Environment

It may be the case that this step does not apply to your project due to regulatory stipulations. For example, it may be necessary to conduct performance testing in a particular lab, supervised by a particular agency. If that is the case for your project, feel free to skip the rest of this step; if not, consider the following.

Load-generation and application-monitoring tools are almost never as easy to engineer as you might expect. Whether issues arise from setting up isolated network environments, procuring hardware, coordinating a dedicated bank of IP addresses for IP spoofing, or establishing version compatibility between monitoring software and server operating systems, there always seem to be issues.

To exacerbate the potential for problems, load-generation tools always lag behind evolving technologies and practices, but that cannot be avoided. Tool creators cannot build in support for every technology, meaning that the vendors will not even start developing support for a particular technology until it has become prominent from their perspective.

This often means that the biggest challenge involved in a performance testing project is getting your first relatively realistic test implemented with users generally being simulated in such a way that the application under test cannot legitimately tell the difference between simulated and real users. Plan for this and do not be surprised when it takes significantly longer than expected to get it all working smoothly.

Activity 7. Implement the Test Design

The details of creating an executable performance test are extremely tool-specific. Regardless of the tool that you are using, creating a performance test typically involves taking a single instance of your test script and gradually adding more instances and/or more scripts over time, thereby increasing the load on the component or system. A single instance of a test script frequently equates to a single simulated or virtual user.

Activity 8. Execute Work Items

When an iteration completes or a delivery is made, the performance testing begins with the highest-priority performance test work item related to that delivery that is reasonable to conduct. At the conclusion of each work item, make your findings available to the team, reprioritize the remaining work items to be conducted during the phase, and then move on to the next-highest-priority execution plan. Whenever possible, limit work item executions to one- to two-days each. By doing so, no time will be lost if the results from a particular work item turn out to be inconclusive, or if the initial test design needs modification in order to produce the intended results.

In general, the keys to performance test work item execution include:

- Analyzing results immediately so you can re-plan accordingly.
- Communicating frequently and openly across the team.
- Recording results and significant findings.
- Recording other data needed to repeat the test later.
- Revisiting performance testing priorities every few days.
- Adapting the test plan and approach as necessary, gaining the appropriate approval for your changes as required.

Activity 9. Report Results and Archive Data

Even though you are sharing data and preliminary results at the conclusion of each work item, it is important to consolidate results, conduct trend analysis, create stakeholder reports, and do collaborative analysis with developers, architects, and administrators before starting the next performance-testing phase. You should allow at least one day between each phase, though you may need more time as the project nears completion. These short analysis and reporting periods are often where the "big breaks" occur. Reporting every few days keeps the team informed, but note that issuing only summary reports rarely tells the whole story.

Part of the job of the performance tester is to find trends and patterns in the data, which can be a very time-consuming endeavor. It also tends to inspire a re-execution of one or more tests to determine if a pattern really exists, or if a particular test was skewed in some way. Teams are often tempted to skip this step to save time. Do not succumb to that temptation; you might end up with more data more quickly, but if you do not stop to look at the data collectively on a regular basis, you are unlikely to know what that data means until it is too late.

As a rule, when a performance test work item is completed, all of the test scripts, test data, test results, environment configurations, and application version information need to be archived for future reference. The method for archiving this information can vary greatly from team to team. If your team does not already have an archival standard, ensure that you include one in your performance test plan.

It is generally acceptable to forgo archiving data related to tests deemed invalid due to obvious mistakes in test setup or execution. Check the compliance criteria that apply to your project. When in doubt, archive the data anyway, but include a note describing the mistake or error.

Activity 10. Modify the Plan and Gain Approval for Modifications

At the completion of each testing phase, it is important to review the performance test plan. Mark the work items that have been completed and evaluate what, if any, cascading effects those completed items have on the plan. For example, consider whether a completed work item eliminates an alternate or exception case for a future phase, or if a planned work item needs to be rescheduled for some reason.

Once you have adjusted the plan, remember to gain approval for the adjustments as required by your process and compliance regulations.

Activity 11. Return to Activity 5

Once the plan has been updated and approved, return to Activity 5 to continue testing with the next delivery, iteration, or checkpoint release. However, that is easier said than done. Sometimes, no matter how hard you try, there are simply no valuable performance testing tasks to conduct at this time. This could be due to environment upgrades, mass re-architecting/refactoring, or other work that someone else needs time to complete. If you find yourself in this situation, make wise use of your time by preparing as much of the final report as you can base on the available information.

Activity 12. Prepare the Final Report

Even after the performance testing is complete and the application has been released for production or for Independent Verification and Validation (IV&V), the job is not done until the final report is completed, submitted to the relevant stakeholders, and accepted. Frequently, these reports are very detailed and well-defined. If you did a good job of determining compliance criteria in activity 1, this should be a relatively straightforward if somewhat detailed and time-consuming task.

Summary

Performance testing in CMMI, auditable, and highly regulated projects entails managing the testing in a highly planned, monitored environment. This type of performance testing is particularly challenging because it is frequently impossible to conduct the next planned activity until you have resolved any defects detected during the previous activity. The key to managing performance testing in such environments is to map work items to the project plan and add details to the plan.

Part III

Identify the Test Environment

In this part:

- Evaluating Systems To Increase Performance Testing Effectiveness

8

Evaluating Systems to Increase Performance Testing Effectiveness

Objectives

- Learn techniques to effectively and efficiently capture the system's functions.
- Learn techniques to effectively and efficiently capture expected user activities.
- Learn techniques to effectively and efficiently capture the system's logical and physical architecture.

Overview

Although system evaluation is an ongoing process throughout the performance testing effort, it offers greater value when conducted early in the test project. The intent of system evaluation is to collect information about the project as a whole, the functions of the system, the expected user activities, the system architecture, and any other details that are helpful in guiding performance testing to achieve the specific needs of the project. This information provides a foundation for collecting the performance goals and requirements, characterizing the workload, creating performance-testing strategies and plans, and assessing project and system risks.

A thorough understanding of the system under test is critical to a successful performance-testing effort. The measurements gathered during later stages are only as accurate as the models that are developed and validated in this stage. The evaluation provides a foundation for determining acceptable performance; specifying performance requirements of the software, system, or component(s); and identifying any risks to the effort before testing even begins.

How to Use This Chapter

Use this chapter to learn how to evaluate systems for a performance-testing effort. The chapter walks you through the main activities involved in system evaluation. To get the most from this chapter:

- Use the "Approach for Evaluating the System" section to get an overview of the activities included in system evaluation, and as quick reference guide for you and your team.

- Use the remaining sections of the chapter to understand the details and critical explanation of system evaluation.

Approach for Evaluating the System

Evaluating the system includes, but is not limited to, the following activities:

- Identify the user-facing functionality of the system.
- Identify non–user-initiated (batch) processes and functions.
- Determine expected user activity.
- Develop a reasonable understanding of potential user activity beyond what is expected.
- Develop an exact model of both the test and production architecture.
- Develop a reasonable model of actual user environments.
- Identify any other process/systems using the architecture.

These activities can be accomplished by following these steps:

- Capture system functions and/or business processes.
- Capture user activities.
- Capture the logical and physical architecture.

These steps are explained in detail in the following sections.

Capture System Functions and/or Business Processes

In this step, you identify the system's core functions to help build the performance acceptance criteria. Subsequently, workload models can be assessed to validate both the acceptance criteria and the collection of system functions.

For performance testing, it is essential to identify the core functions of the system under test. This enables you to make an initial determination of performance acceptance criteria, as well as the user community models used to assess the application's success in meeting these acceptance criteria.

To ensure that all of the system functions are captured, start by meeting with stakeholders to determine the overall purpose of the system or application. Before you can determine how best to test a system, you must completely understand the intent of the system. It is often the case that the project documents do not explicitly express all of the functionality implied by the stakeholders' vision. This is why it is a good idea to start with the stakeholders before moving on to evaluate documentation.

Valuable resources for determining system functionality include:

- Interviews with stakeholders
- Contracts
- Information about how similar applications are used
- Client expectations
- Your own experiences with similar applications
- Design documents
- State transition diagrams
- Requirements and use cases
- Marketing material
- Project plans
- Business cycles
- Key business processes

Considerations

Consider the following key points when capturing system functions and/or business processes:

- Meet with stakeholders to determine the overall purpose of the system.
- Keep in mind that contracts and documentation may deviate from the stakeholders' views of the system. System functions may be user-initiated, scheduled (batch) processes, or processes that are not directly related to the system but nevertheless influence it, such as virus scans and data backups.
- Interviews, documents, and plans frequently contain high-level functions that include a lot of implied functionality. For example, "provide a secure log-in method" implies session tracking, lost password retrieval, new user creation, user identification, user roles, and permissions, and so on.

Capture User Activities

In this step, you identify the key user activities for the application under test. Because it is impractical and virtually impossible to simulate every possible user task or activity in a performance test, you need to decide which activities are most important to simulate. However, before you can do this, you must determine what the possible user activities are.

One place to start is to evaluate the competition's Web site (or application, since competing applications may not be Web-based). Whether or not it is explicitly stated, at some point during the project it is likely to become very obvious that the goal is to allow your users to perform all of the activities available from the competitor. Knowing what these activities are in advance will prevent you from being surprised when they show up in the application—whether or not they appear in any of the documentation.

Valuable resources for determining system functionality include:

- Information about how similar applications are used
- Client expectations
- Your own experiences with similar applications
- Requirements and use cases
- Interviews with stakeholders
- Marketing material
- Help and user documentation
- Client organizational chart
- Network or application security matrix
- Historical data (invoices, Web logs, etc.)
- Major business cycles (monthly calculation, year-end process, five-year archiving, etc.)

Once you have collected a list of what you believe are all the activities a user can perform, circulate the list among the team along with the question, "What else can a user of any type possibly do with this application that isn't on this list?"

Considerations

Consider the following key points when capturing system functions and/or business processes:

- Evaluate the competitor's Web site, since it is likely that keeping up with the competition will eventually become a project goal.
- Remember to take all categories of users into account when soliciting possible user activities. Customers, administrators, vendors, and call-center representatives are likely to use and have access to very different aspects of the application that may not be easily found in the documentation.

- Spend extra time soliciting exception- and error-case activities, which are often implied or buried in documentation.

- If you find activities missing that seem important to you, or that appear in competing applications, consult with the relevant team members as soon as possible. These may indicate unintentional oversights.

Capture the Logical and Physical Architecture

In this step, you identify the relationship between the application and the structure of the hardware and software. This information is critical when you are designing performance tests to address specific areas of concern, and when you are trying to locate a performance bottleneck.

A poor understanding of system architecture can lead to adverse affects on performance testing later in the project and can add time to the tuning process. To capture the logical and physical architecture, the performance tester generally meets with technical stakeholders, architects, and administrators for both the production and test environments. This is critical because designing an effective test strategy requires the performance tester to be aware of which components or tiers of the system communicate with one another and how they do so. It is also valuable to understand the basic structure of the code and contributing external software.

Because the term "architecture" is used in so many different ways by different teams, the following sections have been included for clarity.

Logical Architecture

Logical architecture, as it is used in this chapter, refers to the structure, interaction, and abstraction of software and/or code. That code may include everything from objects, functions, and classes to entire applications. You will have to learn the code-level architecture from your team. When doing so, remember to additionally explore the concept of logical architectural tiers.

The most basic architecture for Web-based applications is known as the *three-tier architecture*, where those tiers often correspond to physical machines with roles defined as follows:

- **Client tier** (the user's machine)—presents requested data.
- **Presentation tier** (the Web server)—handles all business logic and serves data to the client(s).
- **Data storage tier** (the database server)—maintains data used by the system, typically in a relational database.

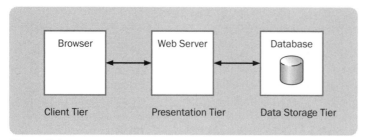

Figure 8.1 *Three-tier Architecture*

More complex architectures may include more tiers, clusters of machines that serve the same role, or even single machines serving as the host for multiple logical tiers.

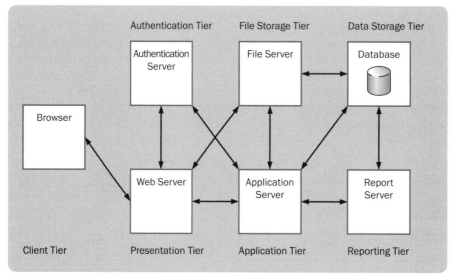

Figure 8.2 *Multi-tier Architecture*

Specifically, this complexity implies the following:

- It is reasonable to think of a logical tier as a grouping of related functions.
- Any tier that is depicted in a logical diagram may span more than one physical machine, share one or more machines with one or more other tiers, or be exclusively tied to a dedicated machine.
- Arrows connecting logical tiers represent a flow of data, not network cables or other physical connections.

One source of confusion is that virtually no one uses terms such as "file storage tier." The "file storage tier" is generally referred to as "the file server," whether or not that tier resides on a dedicated server. The same is true of the presentation tier (Web server), application or business logic tier (application server, often abbreviated as app server), data storage tier (database server), and so on.

Put simply, the key to understanding a logical architecture is that in this type of architecture, each tier contains a unique set of functionality that is logically separated from the other tiers. However, even if a tier is commonly referred to as "server," it is not safe to assume that every tier resides on its own dedicated machine.

Physical Architecture

It should be clear that the physical architecture of the environment—that is, the actual hardware that runs the software—is at least as important as the logical architecture.

Many teams refer to the actual hardware as the "environment" or the "network architecture," but neither term actually encompasses everything of interest to a performance tester. What concerns the tester is generally represented in diagrams where actual, physical computers are shown and labeled with the roles they play, along with the other actual, physical computers with which they communicate. The following diagram shows an example of one such physical architecture diagram.

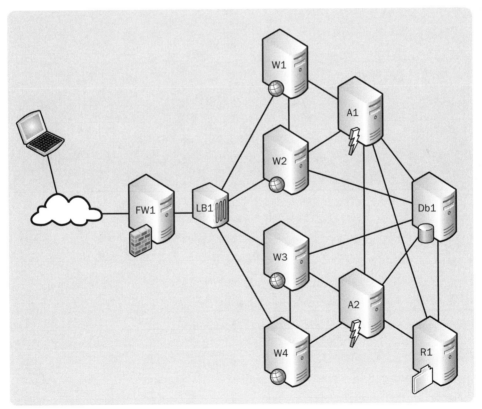

Figure 8.3 *Physical Architecture*

System Architecture

The system architecture is actually just a consolidation of the logical and physical architectures. The diagram below is an example depiction of system architecture. Obviously, it does not include every aspect of the architecture, but it does serve to highlight some points of interest for performance testing, in this case:

- Authentication and application tiers can be served by two servers.
- The mapping will allow information to better design performance tests.
- Performance tests can be targeted at the application tier directly, for example.

Putting these two pieces of the puzzle together adds the most value to the performance-testing effort. Having this information at your fingertips, along with the more detailed code architecture of what functions or activities are handled on which tiers, allows you to design tests that can determine and isolate bottlenecks.

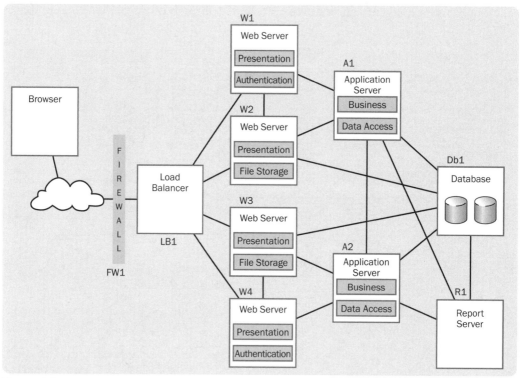

Figure 8.4 *System Architecture*

Considerations

Consider the following key points when capturing the system's logical and physical architecture:

- Some teams view testing as a "black-box" activity; that is, it reminds and educates the team of the necessity to design performance tests well and maintain knowledge of the entire system—from the load-balancing scheme to the thread-sharing model of code objects. Doing so allows the performance tester to identify high risk areas early in the project.

- To test a Web farm, it is necessary to use Internet Protocol (IP) switching techniques to correctly simulate production because of server affinity for IP addresses.

- Application servers and Web servers are frequently multi-homed (that is, having more than one network interface card), with one facing the clients/Web server and another facing the Web server/database back end. This is done for security reasons and also to avoid network utilization on one network interface card for both types of traffic. Characteristics such as this can have a significant impact on performance test design, execution, and analysis.

- The performance tester will not be as effective if he or she is not accepted by the development team as a technical resource. By determining the system architecture, the performance tester can establish him or herself as a technical resource with the developers and architects.

Summary

Although system evaluation is an ongoing process throughout the performance-testing effort, it provides the most value when conducted early in the performance-testing project.

During the system evaluation process, collect information about the project as a whole, the functions of the system and/or business processes, the expected user activities, the system architecture, and any other details that are helpful in guiding performance testing in order to achieve the project's specific needs.

This information helps in defining the performance goals and requirements, characterizing the workload, creating performance test strategies and plans, and assessing project and system risks.

Part IV

Identify Performance Acceptance Criteria

In this part:

- Determining Performance Testing Objective
- Quantifying End-User Response Time Goals
- Consolidating Various Types of Performance Acceptance Criteria

9

Determining Performance Testing Objectives

Objectives

- Learn how to identify and capture performance-testing objectives.
- Learn how to capture or estimate resource usage targets and thresholds.
- Learn how to capture or estimate resource budgets or allocations.
- Learn how to review and update various types of performance-testing objectives and communicate the updates to the team throughout the project as more information becomes available.

Overview

The key to determining the objectives of a performance-testing effort is to identify change, potential risks, and opportunities for improvement. One way to determine and record performance-testing objectives is simply to ask each member of the project team what value you can add or risk you can mitigate for him or her while you are conducting performance testing at a particular point in the project, or immediately following the accomplishment of a particular milestone. Such objectives might include providing data on resource utilization under load, generating specific loads to assist with tuning an application server, or providing a report of the number of objects requested by each Web page.

Although it is most valuable to start collecting performance-testing objectives early in the project life cycle, it is also important to periodically revisit these objectives and ask team members if they would like to see any new objectives added.

Keep in mind the following high-level considerations when determining performance-testing objectives:

- Performance-testing objectives represent the starting point of performance validation and verification activities.

- Performance-testing objectives start with the business entry points: business volume, future growth, and so on. With this information, you can articulate technological objectives mapping to the entry points.

- Performance-testing objectives correlate to business needs and therefore should represent real-world business scenarios involving real customers.

- After you have determined the high-level objectives, you can refine the objectives to map more specifically to the technology.

How to Use This Chapter

Use this chapter to understand how to establish performance-testing objectives in a collaborative manner in order to provide the greatest value to the team. To get the most from this chapter:

- Use the "Terminology" section to understand some common terms related to performance-testing objectives so that you can articulate these terms correctly in the context of your project.

- Use the "Approach for Determining Performance-Testing Objectives" section to get an overview of the approach, and as a quick reference guide for you and your team.

- Use the remaining sections to gain a more detailed understanding of identifying and capturing performance-testing objectives, capturing or estimating resource usage targets and thresholds, and capturing or estimating resource budgets or allocations.

- Use the "Case Studies" section to walk through real-life examples of identifying performance-testing objectives.

Terminology

This chapter uses the following terms.

Term / Concept	Description
Performance-testing objectives	*Performance-testing objectives* refer to data collected through the process of performance testing that is anticipated to have value in determining or improving the quality of the product. However, these objectives are not necessarily quantitative or directly related to a performance requirement, goal, or stated quality of service (QoS) specification.

Term / Concept	Description
Performance objectives	*Performance objectives* are usually specified in terms of response times, throughput (transactions per second), and resource-utilization levels and typically focus on metrics that can be directly related to user satisfaction.
Performance targets	*Performance targets* are the desired values for the metrics identified for your project under a particular set of conditions, usually specified in terms of response time, throughput, and resource-utilization levels. Resource-utilization levels include the amount of processor capacity, memory, disk input/output (I/O), and network I/O that your application consumes. Performance targets typically equate to project goals.
Performance thresholds	*Performance thresholds* are the maximum acceptable values for the metrics identified for your project, usually specified in terms of response time, throughput (transactions per second), and resource-utilization levels. Resource-utilization levels include the amount of processor capacity, memory, disk I/O, and network I/O that your application consumes. Performance thresholds typically equate to requirements.
Performance budgets	*Performance budgets* (sometimes known as *performance allocations*) are constraints placed on developers regarding allowable resource consumption for their component.

Approach for Determining Performance Testing Objectives

Determining performance-testing objectives can be thought of in terms of the following activities:

- Determine the objectives of the performance-testing effort.
- Capture or estimate resource usage targets and thresholds.
- Capture or estimate resource budgets or allocations.
- Identify metrics.
- Communicate results.
- Stay aware of changing objectives, targets, and budgets.

These activities have been discussed in detail in the following sections.

Determine the Objectives of Performance Testing

The methods described in this chapter have proven effective in performance-testing projects. Whether you apply these methods precisely as stated or adapt them to fit your specific project and work environment is unimportant. What is important is to remember that objectives are intentionally collaborative; that is, they are a tool for helping to ensure that the performance-testing effort provides great value to the team—in particular the architects, developers, and administrators—as early as possible in the project life cycle.

Determine Overall Objectives

The first task is to determine the overall objectives for the performance-testing effort. Some common objectives include:

- Determine if the application complies with contracts, regulations, and service level agreements (SLAs).
- Detect bottlenecks to be tuned.
- Assist the development team in determining the performance characteristics for various configuration options.
- Provide input data for scalability and capacity-planning efforts.
- Determine if the application is ready for deployment to production.

Review the Project Plan

Review the project plan with individual team members or small groups. Remember that a project plan does not have to be in the form of a document; for example, it may be a whiteboard sketch, a series of e-mail messages, or a vague idea in the minds of various team members. The point is that no matter how informal the project plan might be, every project has some sort of underlying plan. While reviewing or extracting the plan, whenever you encounter something that looks like a checkpoint, iteration, or milestone, you should ask questions such as:

- What functionality, architecture, and/or hardware will be changing between the last iteration and this iteration?
- Are there performance budgets or thresholds associated with that change? If so, what are they? Can I test them for you? What are the consequences if the budgets or thresholds are not being met?
- Is tuning likely to be required as a result of this change? Are there any metrics that I can collect to help you with the tuning?
- Is this change likely to impact other areas for which we have previously tested/collected metrics? If so, which areas? What tests can I run or what metrics can I collect to help determine if everything is working as expected?
- What risks or significant concerns are related to these changes? What will the consequences be if the changes do not work?

Review the Architecture

Review both the physical and logical architecture with individual team members or small groups. Again, keep in mind that this information may not yet be documented, but someone will at least have a conceptual model in mind — or if they do not, it is probably valuable to find that out as well. As you review or extract the architecture, ask questions such as:

- Have you ever done this/used this before?

- How can we determine if this is performing within acceptable parameters early in the process? Are there experiments or architectural validations that we can use to check some of our assumptions?
- Is this likely to need tuning? What tests can I run or what metrics can I collect to assist in making this determination?

Ask Team Members

Ask individual team members about their biggest performance-related concern(s) for the project and how you could detect these problems as early as possible. You might need to establish trust with team members before you get the best answers. Reassure the team individually and collectively that you are soliciting this information so that you can better assist them in building a high-quality product.

Capture or Estimate Resource Usage Targets and Thresholds

This activity is sometimes misapplied. Remember that targets and thresholds are specific metrics related to particular resources. For example, it is generally agreed that a server's performance degrades significantly if the processor utilization regularly exceeds 80 percent. Based on this, many teams will set a processor utilization target of 70 percent and a threshold of 80 percent. By doing so, you know to alert the team if you observe readings of more than 70-percent processor utilization sustained for more than a few seconds, and to register a defect if a processor utilization rate of more than 80 percent is observed for more than a few seconds. It is worth noting that developing these targets and thresholds can be very time-consuming. Do not continue to set targets and thresholds after their value becomes questionable.

Except in extremely rare circumstances, it is not appropriate for the performance tester to determine targets and thresholds, but only to capture data and compare test results to the targets and thresholds. Even if the performance tester is the most qualified individual to set the targets and thresholds, s/he is not the individual responsible for ensuring that they are met; rather, s/he is responsible for providing information to the team members responsible for ensuring that these targets and thresholds are met so that those persons can make informed decisions. It is important to resist the urge to set targets yourself. Consider the following when performing this activity:

- Talk to the production support team. Determine what they measure and where they set their thresholds. This is their job; they have been doing this for years and they know where the problems occur.
- Ask the architects, or other team members who may be responsible for enforcing and/or making decisions regarding targets and thresholds, to share those decisions with you.

- Find out what the rest of the industry is doing. Even though it is not your job to set targets and thresholds, it is always a good idea to do a Web search or refer to other documentation to find the latest recommendations. If these recommendations seem relevant to your project, make a note of them. This target- and threshold-related data may provide a useful context for the actual data you collect during your testing.

- Work with key performance indicators (network, disk, memory, and processor) for the technology.

- Work with key performance indicators that map to the business requirements. This will help to bridge engineering with the business.

- Work with both key performance indicators and business metrics to better understand the current volume and future growth indicators of the business and the infrastructure.

- Work with the business metrics. Many performance metrics have a strong semantic relationship with the business metrics; for example, database transactions per second and number of orders per second, or number of searches per second with Web hits per second.

- Work with stakeholders when articulating and understanding performance metrics. While most stakeholders are not experts on performance testing, diagnosis, debugging, or analysis, most of them do have expertise in the performance metrics requirements of the business. These stakeholders can articulate metrics around their systems that correlate with the operations. This will facilitate exposing performance metrics in a more intuitive way.

Capture or Estimate Resource Budgets

As mentioned in the previous section, remember that the performance tester's job is to collect and provide information about budgets and allocations, not to enforce them. Determining resource budgets or allocations is one way that teams work together to ensure that targets and thresholds are realistic. For example, if one of your targets is to keep the total RAM usage of a particular server under 1 gigabyte (GB) and that server hosts both a database and application server software, the database software may be given a RAM allocation of 600 megabytes (MB) and the application server software 400 MB. It is the responsibility of the developers and administrators of those software components to stay within those budgets. By making sure that you are aware of these budgets or allocations as a performance tester, you can let the team know when a resource is approaching or exceeding its budget almost immediately, thus giving the team more time to react. Consider the following proven practices when performing this activity:

- Ask the architects, or other team members who may be responsible for enforcing and/or making decisions regarding targets and thresholds, to share those decisions with you.

- Review project documents. Performance testers are not always specifically invited to review design and architecture documents, so remember to ask.
- Attend developer and architect meetings. Take note of comments such as "see if you can get that object under X memory consumption." Although instructions such as these rarely appear on paper, and thus would not be known to you if you didn't attend the meeting, the developer still might appreciate another set of eyes watching his object's memory consumption.
- Work with key performance indicator thresholds that indicate the health of the technologies being used.
- Work with business metrics that indicate whether you are meeting the business requirements; for example, orders per second, number of failed order requests, and so on.

Identify Metrics

Most of the time, this activity is rather transparent. For example, if an objective states that the processor utilization of the Web server should not exceed 80 percent for more than 1 second in 10, it is clear that one metric you should be monitoring is the processor utilization of the Web server, polled at not less than 1-second intervals. You may not want to do this during every test, but there is no question what you need to measure. However, sometimes the associated metrics are not so clear or are not so simple to collect. In these cases, consider the following approach:

- Create a grid or a simple spreadsheet that maps each of the collected objectives to the metric(s) that will indicate if the objective is being met.
- If it is not obvious how to collect each metric without skewing the test or any of the other data you hope to collect at the same time, do some research or work with the development team to determine the optimal approach.
- Collaborate with the developers, architects, and administrators. These parties know which metrics are valuable for their specific purposes and how to capture most of them. Their input will ensure that you know how to put the application in the state that makes those metrics most valuable.
- Consider where you will keep this information and how you will label it so that it is accessible after the tests.

Communicate Results

Communicating the results of tests that capture data related to performance objectives is different than communicating results related to overall performance goals and requirements. Objective-related results are intended to be useful information for the team rather than to determine an application's overall fitness for release. Therefore it is beneficial to share the information freely. In most cases, the fact that an objective is not being met is not something that gets recorded in a defect-tracking system but is simply information to help the team do its job better.

Consider the following techniques when performing this activity:

- Report results versus targets, budgets, and previous measurements as well as your own research. You never know what the team will find most valuable.

- Share reports with the entire team.

- Make the raw data available to the team and invite them to parse it in other ways and to suggest more helpful ways of presenting the data.

- Be ready, willing, interested, and able to re-execute and/or modify the tests as needed.

- Do not send raw data outside the team unless instructed to do so by someone willing and able to take responsibility for any consequences that might arise from doing so.

- Avoid reporting potential causes of poor performance. Instead, report symptoms and conditions. Reporting a cause incorrectly may damage your credibility.

Stay Aware of Changing Objectives, Targets, and Budgets

It is important to remember that objectives are bound to change during the life of a project. As requirements change, features are moved into or out of a particular build, hardware decisions are made, code is refactored, and so on. Performance-testing objectives are bound to change as well. Maintain a running dialogue with your team. Ask the team what is changing and how it impacts the objectives. Whether you do this in person or electronically is up to you; just remember that you will be wasting your own time if you are testing against an old, no-longer-relevant objective.

Case Studies—Identifying Performance-testing Objectives

The following case studies help illustrate the approach to identifying performance-testing objectives.

Case Study 1

Scenario

A 40-year-old financial services company with 3,000 employees is implementing its annual Enterprise Resource Planning (ERP) software upgrade, including new production hardware. The last upgrade resulted in disappointing performance and many months of tuning during production.

Performance Objectives

The performance-testing effort was based on the following overall performance objectives:

- Ensure that the new production hardware is no slower than the previous release.
- Determine configuration settings for the new production hardware.
- Tune customizations.

Performance Budget/Constraints

The following budget limitations constrained the performance-testing effort:

- No server should have sustained processor utilization above 80 percent under any anticipated load. (Threshold)
- No single requested report is permitted to lock more than 20 MB of RAM and 15-percent processor utilization on the Data Cube Server.
- No combination of requested reports is permitted to lock more than 100 MB of RAM and 50-percent processor utilization on the Data Cube Server at one time.

Performance-Testing Objectives

The following priority objectives focused the performance testing:

- Verify that there is no performance degradation over the previous release.
- Verify the ideal configuration for the application in terms of response time, throughput, and resource utilization.
- Resolve existing performance inadequacy with the Data Cube Server.

Questions

The following questions helped to determine relevant testing objectives:

- What is the reason for deciding to test performance?
- In terms of performance, what issues concern you most in relation to the upgrade?
- Why are you concerned about the Data Cube Server?

Case Study 2

Scenario

A financial institution with 4,000 users distributed among the central headquarters and several branch offices is experiencing performance problems with business applications that deal with loan processing.

Six major business operations have been affected by problems related to slowness as well as high resource consumption and error rates identified by the company's IT group. The consumption issue is due to high processor usage in the database, while the errors are related to database queries with exceptions.

Performance Objectives

The performance-testing effort was based on the following overall performance objectives:

- The system must support all users in the central headquarters and branch offices who use the system during peak business hours.
- The system must meet backup duration requirements for the minimal possible timeframe.
- Database queries should be optimal, resulting in processor utilization no higher than 50-75 percent during normal and peak business activities.

Performance Budget/Constraints

The following budget limitations constrained the performance-testing effort:

- No server should have sustained processor utilization above 75 percent under any anticipated load (normal and peak) when users in headquarters and branch offices are using the system. (Threshold)
- When system backups are being performed, the response times of business operations should not exceed 8 percent, or the response times experienced when no backup is being done.
- Response times for all business operations during normal and peak load should not exceed 6 seconds.
- No error rates are allowable during transaction activity in the database that may result in the loss of user-submitted loan applications.

Performance-Testing Objectives

The following priority objectives focused the performance testing:

- Help to optimize the loan-processing applications to ensure that the system meets stated business requirements.
- Test for 100-percent coverage of the entire six business processes affected by the loan-manufacturing applications.

- Target database queries that were confirmed to be extremely sub-optimal, with improper hints and nested sub-query hashing.
- Help to remove superfluous database queries in order to minimize transactional cost.
- Tests should monitor for relevant component metrics: end-user response time, error rate, database transactions per second, and overall processor, memory, network, and disk status for the database server.

Questions

The following questions helped to determine relevant testing objectives:

- What is the reason for deciding to test performance?
- In terms of performance, what issues concern you most in relation to the queries that may be causing processor bottlenecks and transactional errors?
- What business cases related to the queries might be causing processor and transactional errors?
- What database backup operations might affect performance during business operations?
- What are the timeframes for back-up procedures that might affect business operations, and what are the most critical scenarios involved in the time frame?
- How many users are there and where are they located (headquarters, branch offices) during times of critical business operations?

These questions helped performance testers identify the most important concerns in order to help prioritize testing efforts. The questions also helped determine what information to include in conversations and reports.

Case Study 3

Scenario

A Web site is responsible for conducting online surveys with 2 million users in a one-hour timeframe. The site infrastructure was built with wide area network (WAN) links all over the world. The site administrators want to test the site's performance to ensure that it can sustain 2 million user visits in one hour.

Performance Objectives

The performance-testing effort was based on the following overall performance objectives:

- The Web site is able to support a peak load of 2million user visits in a one-hour timeframe.
- Survey submissions should not be compromised due to application errors.

Performance Budget/Constraints

The following budget limitations constrained the performance-testing effort:

- No server can have sustained processor utilization above 75 percent under any anticipated load (normal and peak) during submission of surveys (2 million at peak load).
- Response times for all survey submissions must not exceed 8 seconds during normal and peak loads.
- No survey submissions can be lost due to application errors.

Performance-Testing Objectives

The following priority objectives focused the performance testing:

- Simulate one user transaction scripted with 2 million total virtual users in one hour distributed among two datacenters, with 1 million active users at each data center.
- Simulate the peak load of 2 million user visits in a one-hour period.
- Test for 100-percent coverage of all survey types.
- Monitor for relevant component metrics: end-user response time, error rate, database transactions per second, and overall processor, memory, network and disk status for the database server.
- Test the error rate to determine the reliability metrics of the survey system.
- Test by using firewall and load-balancing configurations.

Questions

The following questions helped to determine relevant testing objectives:

- What is the reason for deciding to test performance?
- In terms of performance, what issues concern you most in relation to survey submissions that might cause data loss or user abandonment due to slow response time?
- What types of submissions need to be simulated for surveys related to business requirements?
- Where are the users located geographically when submitting the surveys?

Summary

Determining and recording performance testing objectives involves communicating with the team to establish and update these objectives as the project advances through milestones. Although it is not always easy to schedule time with each team member—especially when you consider that the project team includes executive stakeholders, analysts, and possibly even representative users—they are generally receptive to sharing information that will help you establish valuable performance-testing objectives. Such objectives might include providing business-related metrics, obtaining resource utilization data under load, generating specific loads to assist with tuning an application server, or providing a report of the number of objects requested by each Web page. While it is most valuable to collect performance-testing objectives early in the project life cycle, it is also important to periodically revisit these objectives and ask team members if they would like to see any new objectives added.

10

Quantifying End-User Response Time Goals

Objectives

- Learn how to identify the difference between performance requirements and performance goals.
- Learn how to apply several methods for capturing subjective performance requirements and goals.

Overview

Ultimately, there is only one end-user response-time metric that matters: the percentage of application users that are frustrated with poor performance. Your application's users do not know or care about the values in your performance test results, how many seconds it takes the screen to display past the user's threshold for "too long," or what the throughput value is. However, users do notice whether the application seems slow—and their impressions can be based on anything from their mood to their prior experience with applications. This chapter describes a method for converting these user perceptions into testable numbers.

Determining what your users will deem "acceptable" in terms of performance can be challenging—and their preferences are subject to significant change over short periods of time. Software-development companies do not want to conduct regular usability studies with groups of representative users because it costs time and money. For the most part, these companies have neither the resources nor the training to conduct usability studies, even if they wanted to.

User experience reports from leading performance testers, shared during peer workshops such as the Workshop on Performance and Reliability (WOPR, *http:// www.performance-workshop.org*), suggest that simply verbalizing your application's performance goals and requirements enables teams to find a way to overcome quantification, technical, logical, logistical, and managerial challenges in order to achieve a successfully performing application. These same performance testers report that quantified goals and requirements are sometimes met, and frequently ignored. Even when they are met, the goals and requirements rarely correlate to satisfied users unless there are also qualitative requirements and goals that serve as a reference point.

How to Use This Chapter

Use this chapter to understand how to establish performance-testing goals and apply several methods for capturing subjective performance requirements and goals. To get the most from this chapter:

- Use the "Terminology" section to understand some common terms used to describe performance-testing goals that will facilitate articulating terms correctly in the context of your project.

- Use the "Approach for Quantifying End-User Response Time" section to get an overview of the approach to determining performance-testing goals, and as quick reference guide for you and your team.

- Use the various activity sections to understand the details of the most critical tasks for quantifying end-user response-time goals.

Terminology

This chapter uses the following terms.

Term / Concept	Description
Performance requirements	*Performance requirements* are those criteria that are absolutely non-negotiable due to contractual obligations, service level agreements (SLAs), or fixed business needs. Any performance criterion that will not unquestionably lead to a decision to delay a release until the criterion passes is not absolutely required—and therefore, not a requirement.
Performance goals	*Performance goals* are the criteria that your team wants to meet before product release, although these criteria may be negotiable under certain circumstances. For example, if a response time goal of three seconds is set for a particular transaction but the actual response time is 3.3 seconds, it is likely that the stakeholders will choose to release the application and defer performance tuning of that transaction for a future release.

Approach for Quantifying End-User Response Time

Quantifying end-user response time goals can be thought of in terms of the following activities:

- Determine application functionality and usage.
- Verbalize and capture performance requirements and goals.
- Quantify performance requirements and goals.
- Record performance requirements and goals.

These activities are discussed in detail in the following sections.

Determine Application Functionality and Usage

Before you can effectively determine the desired performance characteristics of an application, you need to identify the scenarios for which you want to characterize performance. When identifying the business scenarios that have a critical need for performance requirements and goals, it may be useful to think in terms of the following four categories:

- Frequently used scenarios
- Performance-intensive scenarios
- Business-critical scenarios
- Scenarios of special interest (possibly due to contractual obligations or stakeholder visibility)

Once you have identified the scenarios that need performance requirements and/or goals, you can engage the entire team, from executive sponsor to end-user, to determine exactly what those requirements and/or goals should be. In general, all you need to do is get the team to informally tell you how each scenario or group of scenarios should perform. Once you have collected this information, it becomes your job to convert the subjective data into a testable form and then document these testable requirements and/or goals for the purposes of traceability and progress monitoring.

Verbalize and Capture Performance Requirements and Goals

Although it is generally desirable to conduct this activity early in the software development life cycle, it is also valuable to revisit this activity periodically throughout the project. No matter how well you conduct this activity, contracts, perceptions, business drivers, and priorities change as new information becomes available. Keep this in mind as you traverse the project life cycle. For example, if you find out that the terms of a contract have changed while you are presenting what you believe is your final report, it will appear as though your project was never based on the terms of the initial contract.

Throughout this activity, it is important to distinguishing between requirements and goals (see "Terminology" above). Identifying requirements is far from difficult. To determine requirements, focus on contracts and legally binding agreements or standards related to the software under development, and get the executive stakeholders to commit to any performance conditions that will cause them to refuse to release the software into production. The resulting criteria may or may not be related to any specific business scenario or condition. If they are, however, you must ensure that those scenarios or conditions are included in your performance testing.

Performance goals are more challenging to capture and to subsequently quantify, which is why it is important to treat the capture and quantification as separate activities. An extremely common mistake related to performance testing is to begin quantification without first verbalizing the goals subjectively or qualitatively.

Review Project Documentation and Related Contracts

This activity is conceptually straightforward. Regulatory and compliance documents may be challenging to obtain because they often are not readily available for review by non-executives. Even so, it is important to review these standards. The specific language and context of any statement related to testing is critical to determining a compliant process. For example, the difference between "transactions will" and "on average, transactions will" is tremendous. The first case implies that every transaction will comply every single time. The second case is completely ambiguous, as becomes obvious when you try to quantify these criteria.

Frequently, the most important performance-related statements can be found in vision and marketing documents. Vision documents often hold subjective performance goals such as "at least as fast as the previous release," "able to support a growing customer base," and "performance consistent with the market." Marketing documents, however, are notorious for containing unintentional performance requirements.

Any declaration made in a publicly available marketing statement is legally binding in the United States, which makes every claim about performance (or anything else) a non-negotiable requirement. This is not well-known across the software industry and has caused significant challenges when marketing materials included words like "fast," "instant," and "market-leading performance." For each item, the terms must be publicly and reasonably defined and supported—which is where performance testing comes in.

To complete this activity, all you need to do is highlight statements in these published materials that are even loosely related to the application's speed, scalability, and/or stability and set them aside until you are ready to quantify them. Alternatively, you could transpose these statements directly into your requirements-management system just as they are, with the understanding that they are likely to be revised later.

Interview Stakeholders Who Will Influence the "Go Live" Decision

Stakeholders always have an opinion when it comes to performance, and frequently they express those opinions in terms that appear to be already quantified and absolute, although they are rarely well understood. The key to interviewing stakeholders is not only to capture their statements, but also to determine the intent behind those statements.

For example, a stakeholder with a background in telecommunications who may say that she expects the application to have "five 9s of availability" probably does not understand that this equates to the near-impossible standard of a Web site being unavailable for roughly five minutes per year (or roughly one second per day). The truth is that many Web sites could be down for an hour per day, if it is the "right" hour, without customers even noticing.

In fact, it is hard to imagine that Web users would notice a one-second delay, even if it did happen once a day. So while one second of mid-conversation silence each day on a land line is absolutely unacceptable to users, it is probably an unnecessarily strict standard for a Web site. The key is to ask good questions in order to determine the real intent behind statements stakeholders make related to performance. The following are some sample starting questions, along with potential follow-up questions, to help you capture the intent of the stakeholder:

- *How do you expect this application to perform relative to other similar applications/Web sites*? How much better? Ten percent? Noticeably? Dramatically? Which application/Web site in particular exhibits the kind of performance you would like this application/Website to have? You said "x" seconds; how did you decide on that number and what does it indicate to you?

- *How much disruption are you willing to accept due to downtime*? Does that include scheduled maintenance that users are notified about beforehand? Does it matter if the user simply cannot access the Web site/application, or if they are given a message acknowledging that the site is down? What if the users can still accomplish their tasks, but the speed is degraded during downtime?

- *How do you expect the application/Web site to respond to unexpectedly high traffic volumes*? Do you prefer dramatic performance degradation for all users or a "system is temporarily unavailable, please try again later" message for all users in excess of the supported volume? Is it more important to you that the application/Web site demonstrates consistent performance, or variable performance that may be up to 50 percent faster or slower than average based on current usage volume?

To complete this activity, it is most important to record the questions and the answers and not quantify the answers or comment on them unless the stakeholder specifically asks you to explain. The general rule is to ask questions that have answers that do not specifically require quantifications, and to follow up with questions that help you qualify the initial responses subjectively. If the stakeholder does provide numbers, take note of them, but do not assume that they are the right numbers.

Determine If There Are Relevant Standards and/or Competitive Baselines Related to the Application

There are very few performance-related standards outside of safety-critical devices and applications, but there are some. More frequently, market expectations and competition create de facto standards. Every application in every vertical industry will have different methods and sources for determining the competitive landscape. The bottom line: do not assume that you have completely captured goals and requirements until you have checked to see if your application is likely to be compared against an official or de facto standard.

Quantify Performance Requirements and Goals

After capturing the requirements and goals, the next step is to quantify them. While it is not strictly necessary, it is useful to distinguish between requirements and goals prior to quantification. Unlike goals, requirements need to be much more carefully and completely quantified. A goal of "approximately three seconds to render the requested Web page," for example, is a perfectly respectable performance goal, but a completely non-testable performance requirement. Requirements should be specific, such as "the response time must not exceed 10 seconds." Additionally, requirements need to specify the conditions or state of the system to which they apply.

Separate Requirements from Goals

At first glance, this activity seems purely mechanical. If the captured item is legally or contractually binding, or if a stakeholder with the influence to keep the software from being released mandates that an item is required, it is a requirement. The challenge is when an item identified as a requirement is more stringent than other items identified as goals.

In these cases, it is important to bring these conflicting items to stakeholders for additional clarification. It may be the case that the goal is superseded by the requirement—in which case you should simply remove the goal from the list of items. Also, the stakeholders may determine that the requirement is overly aggressive and needs to be modified. Regardless, the sooner these apparent conflicts are resolved, the less confusion they will cause later.

It is worth noting that conflicts between goals and requirements may not become obvious until after both are quantified, making this another important activity to revisit, both after quantification, and periodically during testing to ensure that priorities have not changed.

Quantify Captured Performance Goals

Some goals are at least conceptually easy to quantify. For example, a goal of "no slower than the previous release" is quantified by either referencing the most recent production performance monitoring report, or by executing single-user, light-load, and heavy-load tests against the previous release and recording the results to use as a baseline for comparison. Similarly, to quantify a goal of "at least as fast as our competitors," you can take a series of single-user performance measurements of the competitor's application—perhaps by scheduling a performance test script to execute a common scenario against the application once an hour over a period of a week.

Often, most of the captured goals that need to be quantified are not comparative goals; they are user satisfaction goals, otherwise known as quality of service (QoS) goals. Quantifying end-user satisfaction and/or frustration is more challenging, but far from impossible. To quantify end-user satisfaction, all you need is an application and some representative users. You do not need a completed application; a prototype or demo will do for a first pass at quantification.

For example, with just a few lines of code in the HTML of a demo or prototype, you can control the load time for each page, screen, graphic, control, or list. Using this method, you can create several versions of the application with different response characteristics, then have the users try each, telling you in their own terms whether they find that version unacceptable, slow, reasonable, fast, or whatever descriptors associated with the goals provided to you. Since you know the actual response times, you can then start pairing those numbers to the users' reported degrees of satisfaction. It is not an exact science, but it works well enough for goals—especially if you follow up by asking the same questions about performance testing on the application every time you present those goals. This is applicable for functional testing, user acceptance testing, beta testing, and so on, as you are measuring response times in the background as users interact with the system. This allows you to collect more data and enhance your performance goals as the application evolves.

While quantifying goals, consider distinguishing the goals based on how the application will be used. For instance, a data-entry page that is use 2000 times a day, or a once-a-year comprehensive report on 40 million transactions, will have very different performance goals.

Quantify Captured Performance Requirements

If you are lucky, most of the performance requirements that you captured are already quantified and testable. If you are a little less lucky, the requirements you captured are not quantified at all, in which case you can follow the process described above for quantifying performance goals. If you are unlucky, the performance requirements that you collected are partly quantified and non-testable.

The challenge is that if a requirement is extracted from a contract or existing marketing document, it likely cannot be changed. When you are faced with a requirement such as "three-second average response time," or "2,500 concurrent users," you have to figure out what those requirements mean and what additional information you need in order to make them testable.

There is no absolute formula for this. The basic idea is to interpret the requirements precisely written in common language, supplement them with the most common or expected state for the application, and then get your extended, testable requirement approved by the stakeholder(s). The stakeholders will then be held responsible if someone were to challenge legal compliance with the requirements after the product goes live. To illustrate, consider the following examples:

Requirement: Direct quote from a legal contract: "The Website shall exhibit an average response time of not greater than three (3) seconds."

Extended quantification: This requirement is particularly challenging. The literal, and therefore most likely legal, interpretation is that "Over the life of the Website, the arithmetic mean of all response times, at any point in time, will not exceed 3 seconds." While that is hard enough to determine, response time has not been defined either. Response time could mean "end-user-perceived response time," "server response time," or something else entirely. The following breaks this down systematically:

- Without any information to the contrary, it is probably safe to assume that the only reasonable way to test the three-second average response time is either "with all pages being accessed equally often" or "under the most likely workload distribution."

- Again, without any information to the contrary, you are left to determine the load conditions for the test. In this case, your best bet is probably to average across multiple volumes. For instance, you could get 30 percent of your data from low-load tests, 50 percent from expected-load tests, and 20 percent from high-load tests, and then report a weighted average—assuming that distribution of load is a reasonable approximation of the anticipated production load profile. Alternatively, you could make a case for testing this requirement exclusively under expected load conditions.

Requirement: Direct quote from sales brochure: "This application will support up to 2,500 concurrent users."

Extended quantification: The challenge here is similar because "concurrent user" is not technically accurate for Web applications and therefore can mean several different things.

- Since it is unlikely that you will have the opportunity to determine the intention of the person who chose the term "concurrent," you have to use your best judgment based on the application. Generally, the safest interpretation is "overlapping, active sessions" where an "active session" is one user's activity between the time they access the application until the time they complete their task—without stopping to do something else—whether or not the application technically tracks sessions.

- Using this interpretation, if a user typically has session duration of 15 minutes, statistically, it would take a total of about 5,000 users over a 30-minute period with a realistic ramp-up/ramp-down model to simulate 2,500 overlapping active sessions.

- Also, in this example you have no information about the expected activity of those users. As in the previous example, it is probably safe to assume that the only reasonable way to test this requirement are either "with all pages being accessed equally often" or "under the most likely workload distribution"—although in this case, "under the mostly likely workload distribution" is more likely to be the original author's intent.

See Chapter 12, "Modeling Application Usage" for more information on defining concurrent users.

Record Performance Requirements and Goals

The preferred method for recording goals and requirements will necessarily be particular to your team and tools. However your team manages requirements and goals, you must remember to record both the quantitative and the qualitative versions of the goals and requirements together. By doing so, when it is late in the project and someone tries to decide if the application is performing well enough to be released, you can quickly refer not just to the numbers, but to the intent behind the numbers to help you and your team make a more informed decision.

Summary

Quantifying response-time goals is tightly related to expressing the user's perception of the application's performance. Most often, users of your application are not able to articulate how long it should take to display data onscreen, what the application throughput should be, or how many transactions per second a database must support. However, users do notice the performance behavior of the application, based on their impressions, which are the result of several factors: previous experience, the criticality of the task, and how their expectations have been set.

11

Consolidating Various Types of Performance Acceptance Criteria

Objectives

- Learn how to identify and capture performance requirements and testing objectives based on the perspectives of system users, business owners of the system, and the project team, in addition to compliance expectations and technological considerations.

- Learn how to consolidate this information into a single set of verifiable, complementary performance acceptance criteria.

- Learn how to review and update the performance acceptance criteria throughout the project as more information becomes available.

Overview

Performance requirements and testing objectives are typically derived from five sources: the perspectives of the system users, business owners of the system, and the project team, as well as compliance expectations and technological considerations. This chapter demonstrates how to blend and consolidate the information collected from these sources into a single set of verifiable, complementary performance requirements and testing objectives.

Determining the desired performance characteristics for a system from particular perspectives is only the first part of determining the overall performance acceptance criteria for that system. After examining the desired performance characteristics from limited perspectives, you must resolve those characteristics against one another. For example, end users may desire sub-second response time for every transaction; business stakeholders may want the system to support millions of users; and compliance criteria may mandate strict security policies.

Individually, any of these characteristics may be achievable, but collectively they may not be possible due to time, technology, and/or budget constraints. Finding a way to achieve these desired characteristics presents team-wide challenges that should be addressed proactively, not reactively after conflicts become apparent through testing.

How to Use This Chapter

Use this chapter to understand how to consolidate various types of performance acceptance criteria based on the perspectives of system users, business owners of the system, and the project team, and on compliance expectations and the technologies involved. To get the most from this chapter:

- Use the "Terminology" section to understand common terms used in relation to performance-testing requirements and acceptance criteria that will facilitate articulating terms correctly in the context of your project.

- Use the "Approach for Consolidating Acceptance Criteria" section to get an overview of the approach to determining performance testing acceptance criteria, and as quick reference guide for you and your team.

- Use the various activity sections to understand the details of consolidating acceptance criteria based on the perspectives of system users, business owners of the system, and the project team, and on compliance expectations and technological considerations.

Terminology

The following terms and definitions help to distinguish between the various types of performance characteristics.

Term / Concept	Description
Performance requirements	*Performance requirements* are those criteria that are absolutely non-negotiable due to contractual obligations, service level agreements (SLAs), or fixed business needs. Any performance criterion that will not unquestionably lead to a decision to delay a release until the criterion passes is not absolutely required—and therefore, not a requirement.
Performance goals	*Performance goals* are the criteria that your team wants to meet before product release, although these criteria may be negotiable under certain circumstances. For example, if a response time goal of three seconds is set for a particular transaction but the actual response time is 3.3 seconds, it is likely that the stakeholders will choose to release the application and defer performance tuning of that transaction for a future release.

Term / Concept	Description
Performance thresholds	*Performance thresholds* are the maximum acceptable values for the metrics identified for your project, usually specified in terms of response time, throughput (transactions per second), and resource-utilization levels. Resource-utilization levels include the amount of processor capacity, memory, disk I/O, and network I/O that your application consumes. Performance thresholds typically equate to requirements.
Performance targets	*Performance targets* are the desired values for the metrics identified for your project under a particular set of conditions, usually specified in terms of response time, throughput, and resource-utilization levels. Resource-utilization levels include the amount of processor capacity, memory, disk I/O, and network I/O that your application consumes. Performance targets typically equate to project goals.
Performance testing objectives	*Performance testing objectives* refer to data collected through the performance-testing process that is anticipated to have value in determining or improving product quality. However, these objectives are not necessarily quantitative or directly related to a performance requirement, goal, or stated quality of service (QoS) specification.

Approach for Consolidating Acceptance Criteria

Consolidating acceptance criteria can be thought of in terms of the following activities:

- Investigate end-user requirements.
- Collect business requirements.
- Determine technical requirements.
- Research standards, compliance, and contracts.
- Establish performance-testing objectives.
- Compare and consolidate performance characteristics.
- Review and update the performance plan.

These activities are discussed in detail in the following sections.

Investigate End-User Requirements

Once your application reaches production, the most important performance characteristic that matters is that application users must not be frustrated with poor performance. If users are annoyed, they will find an alternative to your application. If they do become frustrated, it will not matter how many users your application supports, how much data it can process, or how efficient it is in its use of resources—in fact, even if you accomplished all of the above and were the first to market the application with the new features, it will still mean nothing to the user.

Users of your application will not know or care about the results of the performance tests, how many seconds it takes the screen to display past a user's normal threshold for "too long," or what the throughput is. Primarily, application users notice only whether the application seems slow or not. Also, users' reactions (or not) can be based on anything, including how they feel at the time or their overall experience with applications.

Quantifying end-user satisfaction and/or frustration can be challenging but is far from impossible. To quantify end-user satisfaction, all you need is an application and some representative users. You do not need a completed application, since a prototype or demo will suffice for a first pass. For example, with only a few lines of code in the HTML of a demo or prototype, you can control the load time for each page, screen, graphic, control, or list. Using this method, you can create several versions of the application with different response characteristics. You can then ask users to try each version and tell you whether they find that version unacceptable, slow, reasonable, fast, or whatever terms correspond to the captured goals.

Because you know the actual response times, you can start equating those numbers to the users' reported degrees of satisfaction. This is not an exact science, but it generally works well for goals—especially if you follow up by asking the same questions about the application's performance each time you test it. This applies for functional testing, user acceptance testing, beta testing, or any other reason, as you are measuring response times in the background as testers interact with the system. This approach allows you to collect more data and enhance your end-user performance goals as the application evolves.

Collect Business Requirements

The real engineering challenge is not only being able to meet your business requirements, but also achieving them on time and within budget. Before you can find this balance, you must first determine those business requirements. For example, you will need to determine the budget for new hardware, and what existing hardware is available. You will need to know how rigid the target delivery date is, whether an initial release to a limited number of users is acceptable, and what project aspects take priority. For instance, if a situation arises where you can achieve the desired performance on time and on budget by eliminating valuable features, you must ask yourself whether that tradeoff is worth considering.

Creating a performance plan—not a performance test plan, but an overall plan for achieving desired performance characteristics—is the process most teams use to demonstrate how to spend the technical and financial performance budget in order to create the desired experiences, and to determine the overall cost of that performance in terms of dollars, resources, and schedule. Some areas worthy of significant consideration in a performance plan include:

- Throughput and latency (e.g., do you need to ensure that deploying this application will not adversely affect other applications that use the same network?)
- Responsiveness (e.g., are there components of your application that need to interact in a timely manner, such as a load balancer that skips a particular Web server if it does not respond in <200 milliseconds?)
- Capacity (e.g., can you afford the infrastructure to support up to 500 users under standard conditions?)
- Cost of entry (e.g., is it viable to achieve the end-user requirements with existing hardware?)

You may also be affected by external business requirements in addition to the internal requirements. An example of an external business requirement is achieving performance characteristics that are "as good as or better than" competing applications. Every application in every vertical industry will have different methods and sources for determining its competitive landscape. Even if you cannot run load tests against a competitor, you can still collect valuable response time information by, for example, periodically surfing the site and from researching sites such as www.keynote.com.

The bottom line: do not assume that your site will not be compared against others simply because there is no published standard; de-facto standards are more likely to set your users' expectations than formal metrics do.

Determine Technical Requirements

Usually, technical performance characteristics only indirectly relate to the other categories of requirements. These characteristics frequently concern the use of particular technologies, and usually consist of targets and thresholds that are specific metrics related to particular resources.

For example, it is generally agreed that once a server's processor utilization reaches 80 percent, user requests will start to significantly queue, and therefore users will experience poor service even though the server might still be running fine. Based on this, many teams will set a processor utilization target of 70 percent and a threshold of 80 percent. By doing so, they are telling the performance tester to alert the team if he or she observes readings of more than 70-percent processor utilization sustained for more than a few seconds, and to register a defect if a processor utilization rate of more than 80 percent is observed for more than a few seconds under the target workloads.

Capturing and managing technical performance-testing requirements generally requires that you:

- **Determine objectives of performance testing.** This activity ensures that technical requirements are prioritized appropriately for the performance concerns of the project.

- **Capture or estimate resource usage targets and thresholds.** These may come from architects, administrators, design documents, or hardware/software technical documentation.

- **Capture or estimate resource budgets or allocations.** Typically assigned to developers by architects and administrators, these represent the amount of a specific resource a particular component may use so that the system as a whole will not violate its targets or thresholds.

- **Identify metrics.** There is often more than one way to measure resource consumption. The team must agree on the specific method and metric for each technical requirement to enable communication and understanding.

- **Communicate results.** Collected data that relates to technical requirements is valuable to various members of the team in different forms as soon as it is available. Sharing the data immediately assists with design, tuning, and identifying requirements that may need to be revisited.

- **Keep abreast of changing objectives, targets, and budgets.** Just like other types of requirements, technical requirements are bound to change during the course of the project. Expect this and keep up with the changes.

Research Standards, Compliance, and Contracts

The performance characteristics in this category are frequently the least negotiable, whether or not they have a significant impact on end-user satisfaction, budget, schedule, or technology. Determining performance requirements in this category generally involves the following tasks:

- Obtaining documents and standards that spell out legally enforceable performance requirements.

- Interpreting those legally enforceable performance requirements within the context of your project.

- Determining if any de facto standards or competitive comparisons apply to your project. If so, collect the relevant data.

- Getting stakeholder approval for the interpretations. Because the company or even individual stakeholders could be held legally liable if the application does not meet the requirements, this is a situation where stakeholder approval is highly recommended.

Establish Performance-Testing Objectives

Determining performance-testing objectives can be fairly easy. The challenge is that the performance tester does not always have easy access to either explicit or implied objectives, and therefore frequently must conduct a systematic search for these objectives. Determining performance-testing objectives generally involves the following tasks:

- Determining the overall objectives for the performance testing effort, such as:
  - Detect bottlenecks that need tuning.
  - Assist the development team in determining the performance characteristics for various configuration options.
  - Provide input data for scalability and capacity-planning efforts.
- Reviewing the project plan with individual team members or small groups. Ask questions such as:
  - What functionality, architecture, and/or hardware will be changing between the last iteration and this iteration?
  - Is tuning likely to be required as a result of this change? Are there any metrics that I can collect to help you with the tuning?
  - Is this change likely to impact other areas for which we have previously tested/collected metrics?
- Reviewing both the physical and logical architecture with individual team members or small groups. As you review the architecture, ask questions such as:
  - Have you ever done this/used this before?
  - How can we determine early in the process if this is performing within acceptable parameters?
  - Is this likely to need tuning? What tests can I run or what metrics can I collect to assist in making this determination?
- Asking individual team members about their biggest performance-related concern(s) for the project and how you could detect those problems as early as possible.

While it is most valuable to collect performance testing objectives early in the project life cycle, it is also important to periodically revisit these objectives and ask team members if they would like to see any new objectives added.

Compare and Consolidate Performance Characteristics

After you have identified performance characteristics from each of these categories, it is important to compare and consolidate them. Often, the best way to do so is to employ a cross-functional team while developing or enhancing the performance plan. Some of the key discussions, activities, and tradeoffs to consider include:

- Determining the technical characteristics necessary to achieve end-user and compliance requirements.

- Comparing the technical characteristics necessary to achieve end-user and compliance requirements to the technical requirements you have already collected. Make note of significant differences that impact the project.

- Estimating the cost—in terms of schedule, resources, and dollars—of achieving the revised technical requirements.

- Reviewing the overall objectives for conducting performance testing to determine if those testing objectives support the technical requirements and business needs.

The key here is to focus on the experience you are trying to create, and from that, determine the associated costs of achieving that experience. In many cases this can lead to reverse-engineering desired end-user performance characteristics into actionable technical requirements, and then extrapolating those technical requirements into such relevant costs as time and money.

Review and Update the Performance Plan

As with many aspects of software development, the performance plan is a moving target. The previous six activities, if you accomplish them early in the development life cycle, will likely lead to a tentative application design that can be evaluated against technical and business requirements. As long as that design continues to make sense when evaluated against the requirements, stick with it and flesh it out incrementally as you go. When that design stops making sense when evaluated against the requirements, recalibrate until it does make sense.

You are likely to iterate through this process many times throughout the development cycle, each time potentially updating the application design, the performance plan, and the performance requirements. Do not try to flesh it out all at once, and do not expect perfection. The key is to keep the design, the plan, and the requirements in sync and moving together to achieve satisfied end users and happy stakeholders once the application goes live.

Summary

Performance requirements and testing objectives are typically derived from the perspectives of system users, business owners, and the project team, as well as compliance expectations and technological considerations.

To have confidence in the completeness of your system acceptance criteria, they should be based on the information collected from all these different perspectives, which should result in a single set of verifiable, complementary performance requirements and testing objectives.

It is important to always keep in mind that the performance characteristic that matters most is that application users must not be frustrated with poor performance.

Part V
Plan and Design Tests

In this part:
- Modeling Application Usage
- Determining Individual User Data and Variances

12

Modeling Application Usage

Objectives

- Learn the difference between concurrent users and user sessions and why this is important when defining input for Web load tests.
- Learn how to identify individual usage scenarios.
- Learn about the metrics that will help in developing realistic workload characterizations.
- Learn how to incorporate individual usage scenarios and their variances into user groups.
- Learn how to identify and model special considerations when blending groups of users into single models.
- Learn how to construct realistic workload models for Web applications based on expectations, documentation, observation, log files, and other data available prior to the release of the application to production.

Overview

The most common purpose of Web load tests is to simulate the user's experience as realistically as possible. For performance testing to yield results that are directly applicable to understanding the performance characteristics of an application in production, the tested workloads must represent a real-world production scenario. To create a reasonably accurate representation of reality, you must understand the business context for the use of the application, expected transaction volumes in various situations, expected user path(s) by volume, and other usage factors. By focusing on groups of users and how they interact with the application, this chapter demonstrates an approach to developing workload models that approximate production usage based on various data sources.

Testing a Web site in such a way that the test can reliably predict performance is often more art than science. As critical as it is to creating load and usage models that will predict performance accurately, the data necessary to create these models is typically not directly available to the individuals who conduct the testing. When it is, it is typically not complete or comprehensive.

While it is certainly true that simulating unrealistic workload models can provide a team with valuable information when conducting performance testing, you can only make accurate predictions about performance in a production environment, or prioritize performance optimizations, when realistic workload models are simulated.

How to Use This Chapter

Use this chapter to understand how to model workload characterization, which can be used for performance testing to simulate production characteristics. To get the most from this chapter:

- Use the "Approach for Modeling Application Usage" section to get an overview of the approach for modeling workload characterization and as a quick reference guide for you and your team.

- Use the various activity sections to understand the details of the activities, and to find critical explanations of the concepts of user behavior involved in workload modeling.

Approach for Modeling Application Usage

The process of identifying one or more composite application usage profiles for use in performance testing is known as *workload modeling*. Workload modeling can be accomplished in any number of ways, but to varying degrees the following activities are conducted, either explicitly or implicitly, during virtually all performance-testing projects that are successful in predicting or estimating performance characteristics in a production environment:

- Identify the objectives.
- Identify key usage scenarios.
- Determine navigation paths for key scenarios.
- Determine individual user data and variances.
- Determine the relative distribution of scenarios.
- Identify target load levels.
- Prepare to implement the model.

These activities are discussed in detail in the following sections.

Identify the Objectives

The objectives of creating a workload model typically center on ensuring the realism of a test, or on designing a test to address a specific requirement, goal, or performance-testing objective. (For more information, see Chapter 9, "Determine Performance Testing Objectives" and Chapter 10, "Quantify End-User Response Time Goals.") When identifying the objectives, work with targets that will satisfy the stated business requirements. Consider the following key questions when formulating your objectives:

- What is the current or predicted business volume over time? For example, how many orders are typically placed in a given time period, and what other activities— number of searches, browsing, logging, and so on—support order placement?

- How is the business volume expected to grow over time? Your projection should take into account future needs such as business growth, possible mergers, introduction of new products, and so on.

- What is the current or predicted peak load level? This projection should reflect activities that support sales and other critical business processes, such as marketing campaigns, newly shipped products, time-sensitive activities such as stock exchange transactions dependent on external markets, and so on.

- How quickly do you expect peak load levels to be reached? Your prediction should take into consideration unusual surges in business activity—how fast can the organization adjust to the increased demand when such an event happens?

- How long do the peak load levels continue? That is, how long does the new demand need to be sustained before exhaustion of a resource compromises the service level agreements (SLAs)? For example, an economic announcement may cause the currency-exchange market to experience prolonged activity for two or three days, as opposed to just a few hours.

This information can be gathered from Web server logs, marketing documentation reflecting business requirements, or stakeholders. The following are some of the objectives identified during this process:

- Ensure that one or more models represent the peak expected load of X orders being processed per hour.

- Ensure that one or more models represent the difference between "quarterly close-out" period usage patterns and "typical business day" usage patterns.

- Ensure that one or more models represent business/marketing projections for up to one year into the future.

It is acceptable if these objectives only make sense in the context of the project at this point. The remaining activities will help you fill in the necessary details to achieve the objectives.

Considerations

Consider the following key points when identifying objectives:

- Throughout the process of creating workload models, remember to share your assumptions and drafts with the team and solicit their feedback.

- Do not get overly caught up in striving for perfection, and do not fall into the trap of oversimplification. In general, it is a good idea to start executing tests when you have a testable model and then enhance the model incrementally while collecting results.

Determine Key Usage Scenarios

To simulate every possible user task or activity in a performance test is impractical, if not a sheer impossibility. As a result, no matter what method you use to identify key scenarios, you will probably want to apply some limiting heuristic to the number of activities or key scenarios you identify for performance testing. You may find the following limiting heuristics useful:

- Include contractually obligated usage scenario(s).
- Include usage scenarios implied or mandated by performance testing goals and objectives.
- Include most common usage scenario(s).
- Include business-critical usage scenario(s).
- Include performance-intensive usage scenario(s).
- Include usage scenarios of technical concern.
- Include usage scenarios of stakeholder concern.
- Include high-visibility usage scenarios.

The following information sources are frequently useful in identifying usage scenarios that fit into the categories above:

- Requirements and use cases
- Contracts
- Marketing material
- Interviews with stakeholders
- Information about how similar applications are used
- Observing and asking questions of beta-testers and prototype users
- Your own experiences with how similar applications are used

If you have access to Web server logs for a current implementation of the application—whether it is a production implementation of a previous release, a representative prototype, or a beta release—you can use data from those logs to validate and/or enhance the data collected using the resources above.

After you have collected a list of what you believe are the key usage scenarios, solicit commentary from the team members. Ask what they think is missing, what they think can be de-prioritized, and, most importantly, why. What does not seem to matter to one person may still be critical to include in the performance test. This is due to potential side effects that activity may have on the system as a whole, and the fact that the individual who suggests that the activity is unimportant may be unaware of the consequences.

Considerations

Consider the following key points when determining key usage scenarios:

- Whenever you test a Web site with a significant amount of new features/functionality, use interviews. By interviewing the individuals responsible for selling/marketing the new features, you will find out what features/functions will be expected and therefore most likely to be used. By interviewing existing users, you can determine which of the new features/functions they believe they are most likely to use.

- When testing a pre-production Web site, the best option is to roll out a (stable) beta version to a group of representative users (roughly 10-20 percent the size of the expected user base) and analyze the log files from their usage of the site.

- Run simple in-house experiments using employees, customers, clients, friends, or family members to determine, for example, natural user paths and the page-viewing time differences between new and returning users. This method is a highly effective method of data collection for Web sites that have never been live, as well as a validation of data collected by using other methods.

- Remember to ask about usage by various user types, roles, or personas. It is frequently the case that team members will not remember to tell you about the less common user types or roles if you do not explicitly ask.

- Think about system users and batch processes as well as human end users. For example, there might be a batch process that runs to update the status of orders while users are performing activities in the site. Be sure to account for those processes because they might be consuming resources.

- For the most part, Web servers are very good at serving text and graphics. Static pages with average-size graphics are probably less critical than dynamic pages, forms, and multimedia pages.

- Think about nonhuman system users and batch processes as well as end users. For example, there might be a batch process that runs to update the status of orders while users are performing activities on the site. In this situation, you would need to account for those processes because they might be consuming resources.

- For the most part, Web servers are very effective at serving text and graphics. Static pages with average-size graphics are probably less critical than dynamic pages, forms, and multimedia pages.

Determine Navigation Paths for Key Scenarios

Now that you have a list of key scenarios, the next activity is to determine how individual users actually accomplish the tasks or activities related to those scenarios.

Human beings are unpredictable, and Web sites commonly offer redundant functionality. Even with a relatively small number of users, it is almost certain that real users will not only use every path you think they will to complete a task, but they also will inevitably invent some that you had not planned. Each path a user takes to complete an activity will put a different load on the system. That difference may be trivial, or it may be enormous—there is no way to be certain until you test it. There are many methods to determine navigation paths, including:

- Identifying the user paths within your Web application that are expected to have significant performance impact and that accomplish one or more of the identified key scenarios

- Reading design and/or usage manuals

- Trying to accomplish the activities yourself

- Observing others trying to accomplish the activity without instruction

After the application is released for unscripted user acceptance testing, beta testing, or production, you will be able to determine how the majority of users accomplish activities on the system under test by evaluating Web server logs. It is always a good idea to compare your models against reality and make an informed decision about whether to do additional testing based on the similarities and differences found.

Apply the same limiting heuristics to navigation paths as you did when determining which paths you wanted to include in your performance simulation, and share your findings with the team. Ask what they think is missing, what they think can be de-prioritized, and why.

Considerations

Consider the following key points when determining navigation paths for key scenarios:

- Some users will complete more than one activity during a visit to your site.
- Some users will complete the same activity more than once per visit.
- Some users may not actually complete any activities during a visit to your site.
- Navigation paths are often easiest to capture by using page titles.
- If page titles do not work or are not intuitive for your application, the navigation path may be easily defined by steps the user takes to complete the activity.
- First-time users frequently follow a different path to accomplish a task than users experienced with the application. Consider this difference and what percentage of new versus return user navigation paths you should represent in your model.
- Different users will spend different amounts of time on the site. Some will log out, some will close their browser, and others will leave their session to time out. Take these factors into account when determining or estimating session durations.
- When discussing navigation paths with your team or others, it is frequently valuable to use visual representations.

Example Visual Representation

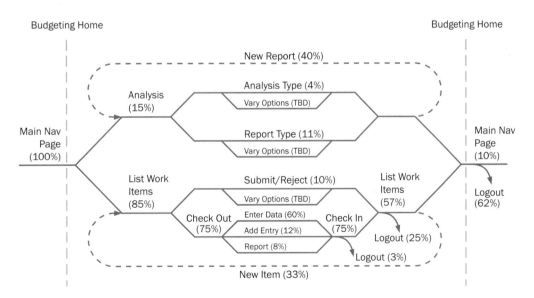

Figure 12.1 *Workload for Key Scenarios*

Determine Individual User Data and Variances

No matter how accurate the model representing navigation paths and usage scenarios is, it is not complete without accounting for the data used by and the variances associated with individual users. While thinking of users as interchangeable entities leads to tests being simpler to design and analyze, and even makes some classes of performance issues easier to detect, it masks much of the real-world complexity that your Web site is likely to encounter in production. Accounting for and simulating this complexity is crucial to finding the performance issues most likely to be encountered by real users, as well as being an essential element to making any predictions or estimations about performance characteristics in production.

The sections that follow detail some of the sources of information from which to model individual user data and variances, and some of the data and variances that are important to consider when creating your model and designing your tests.

Web Site Metrics in Web Logs

For the purposes of this chapter, Web site metrics are the variables that help you understand a site's traffic and load patterns from the server's perspective. Web site metrics are generally averages that may vary with the flow of users accessing the site, but they generally provide a high-level view of the site's usage that is helpful in creating models for performance testing. These metrics ultimately reside in the Web server logs. (There are many software applications that parse these logs to present these metrics graphically or otherwise, but these are outside of the scope of this chapter.) Some of the more useful metrics that can be read or interpreted from Web server logs (assuming that the Web server is configured to keep logs) include:

- **Page views per period.** A *page view* is a page request that includes all dependent file requests (.jpg files, CSS files, etc). Page views can be tracked over hourly, daily, or weekly time periods to account for cyclical patterns or bursts of peak user activity on the Web site.

- **User sessions per period.** A *user session* is the sequence of related requests originating from a user visit to the Web site, as explained previously. As with page views, user sessions can span hourly, daily, and weekly time periods.

- **Session duration.** This metric represents the amount of time a user session lasts, measured from the first page request until the last page request is completed. Session duration takes into account the amount of time the user pauses when navigating from page to page.

- **Page request distribution.** This metric represents the distribution, in percentages, of page hits according to functional types (Home, login, Pay, etc.). The distribution percentages will establish a weighting ratio of page hits based on the actual user utilization of the Web site.

- **Interaction speed.** This metric represents the time users take to transition between pages when navigating the Web site, constituting the think time behavior. It is important to remember that every user will interact with the Web site at a different rate.

- **User abandonment.** This metric represents the length of time that users will wait for a page to load before growing dissatisfied and exiting the site. Sessions that are abandoned are quite normal on the Internet and consequently will have an impact on the load test results.

Determine the Relative Distribution of Scenarios

Having determined which scenarios to simulate and what the steps and associated data are for those scenarios, and having consolidated those scenarios into one or more workload models, you now need to determine how often users perform each activity represented in the model relative to the other activities needed to complete the workload model.

Sometimes one workload distribution is not enough. Research and experience have shown that user activities often vary greatly over time. To ensure test validity, you must validate that activities are evaluated according to time of day, day of week, day of month, and time of year. As an example, consider an online bill-payment site. If all bills go out on the 20th of the month, the activity on the site immediately before the 20th will be focused on updating accounts, importing billing information, and so on by system administrators, while immediately after the 20th, customers will be viewing and paying their bills until the payment due date of the 5th of the next month. The most common methods for determining the relative distribution of activities include:

- Extract the actual usage, load values, common and uncommon usage scenarios (user paths), user delay time between clicks or pages, and input data variance (to name a few) directly from log files.

- Interview the individuals responsible for selling/marketing new features to find out what features/functions are expected and therefore most likely to be used. By interviewing existing users, you may also determine which of the new features/ functions they believe they are most likely to use.

- Deploy a beta release to a group of representative users (roughly 10-20 percent the size of the expected user base) and analyze the log files from their usage of the site.

- Run simple in-house experiments using employees, customers, clients, friends, or family members to determine, for example, natural user paths and the page-viewing time differences between new and returning users.

- As a last resort, you can use your intuition, or best guess, to make estimations based on your own familiarity with the site.

Teams and individuals use a wide variety of methods to consolidate individual usage patterns into one or more collective models. Some of those include spreadsheets, pivot tables, narrative text, Unified Modeling Language (UML) collaboration diagrams, Markov Chain diagrams, and flow charts. In each case the intent is to make the model as a whole easy to understand, maintain, and communicate across the entire team.

One highly effective method is to create visual models of navigation paths and the percentage of users you anticipate will perform each activity that are intuitive to the entire team, including end users, developers, testers, analysts, and executive stake-holders. The key is to use language and visual representations that make sense to your team without extensive training. In fact, visual models are best when they convey their intended meaning without the need for any training at all. After you create such a model, it is valuable to circulate that model to both users and stakeholders for review/comment. Following the steps taken to collect key usage scenarios, ask the team members what they think is missing, what they think can be de-prioritized, and why. Often, team members will simply write new percentages on the visual model, making it very easy for everyone to see which activities have achieved a consensus, and which have not.

Once you are confident that the model is appropriate for performance testing, supplement that model with the individual usage data collected for each navigation path during the "Determine Individual User Data and Variances" activity, in such a way that the model contains all the data you need to create the actual test.

Activity

Member Login

	Min	Max	Std	Distribution	
Think Time (sec)	6.0	18.0	2.0	Normal	
	Min	Max	Std	Distribution	Event
Abandon (sec)	20.0	50.0	N/A	Linear	Repeat
Pass/Fail Condition	If fail, log data and repeat one time.				
	Field	Variable Name	Data Description	Data Location	
Credentials	Username	str_guid	Valid Usernames	Datapool	
	Password	str_pwd	Valid Passwords	Datapool	

Create Account

	Min	Max	Std	Distribution	
Think Time (sec)	25.0	60.0	8.0	Normal	
	Min	Max	Std	Distribution	Event
Abandon (sec)	60.0	120.0	N/A	NegExp	Abandon
Pass/Fail Condition	If fail, log data and abandon user.				
	Field	Variable Name	Data Description	Data Location	
Acct Data	Ccard	int_ccard	Valid C-card #s	File.csv	
	Exp_date	int_exp	Valid E-date for C-card	File.csv	
	Name	str_name	Valid Name for C-card	File.csv	
	Street	str_street	Valid Street for C-card	File.csv	
	City	str_city	Valid City for C-card	File.csv	
	State	str_state	Valid State for C-card	File.csv	
	Zip	str_zip	Valid Zip for C-card	File.csv	

Sync Point

Home Page

Type	Parameter(s)
Navigational	None

Condition

In Stock?

Criteria	Resulting Activity(s)
Yes	Purchase
No	Exit

Figure 12.2 *Visual Model of Navigation Paths*

Considerations

Consider the following key points when determining the relative distribution of scenarios:

- Create visual models and circulate them to users and stakeholders for review/ comment.

- Ensure that the model is intuitive to nontechnical users, technical designers, and everyone in between.

- Because performance tests frequently consume large amounts of test data, ensure that you include enough in your data files.

- Ensure that the model contains all of the supplementary data necessary to create the actual test.

Identify Target Load Levels

A customer visit to a Web site comprises a series of related requests known as a user session. Users with different behaviors who navigate the same Web site are unlikely to cause overlapping requests to the Web server during their sessions. Therefore, instead of modeling the user experience on the basis of concurrent users, it is more useful to base your model on user sessions. User sessions can be defined as a sequence of actions in a navigational page flow, undertaken by a customer visiting a Web site.

Quantifying the Volume of Application Usage: Theory

It is frequently difficult to determine and express an application's usage volume because Web-based multi-user applications communicate via stateless protocols. Although terms such as "concurrent users" and "simultaneous users" are frequently used, they can be misleading when applied to modeling user visits to a Web site. In Figures 12.3 and 12.4 below, each line segment represents a user activity, and different activities are represented by different colors. The solid black line segment represents the activity "load the Home page." User sessions are represented horizontally across the graph. In this hypothetical representation, the same activity takes the same amount of time for each user. The time elapsed between the Start of Model and End of Model lines is one hour.

Server Perspective of User Activities

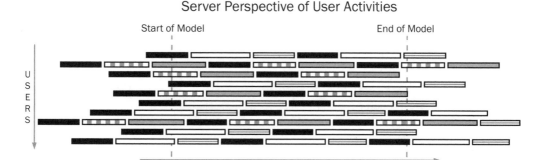

Figure 12.3 *Server Perspective of User Activities*

Figure 12.3 above represents usage volume from the perspective of the server (in this case, a Web server). Reading the graph from top to bottom and from left to right, you can see that user 1 navigates first to page "solid black" and then to pages "white," "polka dot," "solid black," "white," and "polka dot." User 2 also starts with page "solid black," but then goes to pages "zebra stripe," "grey," etc. You will also notice that virtually any vertical slice of the graph between the start and end times will reveal 10 users accessing the system, showing that this distribution is representative of 10 concurrent, or simultaneous, users. What should be clear is that the server knows that 10 activities are occurring at any moment in time, but not how many actual users are interacting with the system to generate those 10 activities.

Figure 12.4 below depicts another distribution of activities by individual users that would generate the server perspective graph above.

Actual Distribution of User Activities Over Time

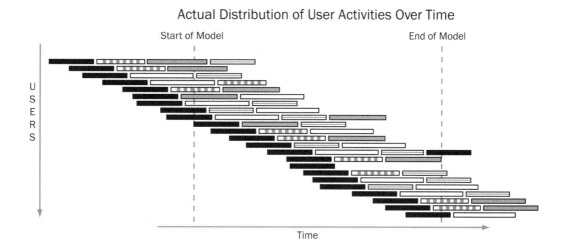

Figure 12.4 *Actual Distribution of User Activities Over Time*

In this graph, the activities of 23 individual users have been captured. Each of these users conducted some activity during the time span being modeled, and their respective activities can be thought of as 23 user sessions. Each of the 23 users began interacting with the site at a different time. There is no particular pattern to the order of activities, with the exception of all users who started with the "solid black" activity. These 23 users actually represent the exact same activities in the same sequence shown in Figure 12.3. However, as depicted in Figure 12.4, at any given time there are 9 to 10 concurrent users. The modeling of usage for the above case in terms of volume can be thought of in terms of total hourly users, or user sessions counted between "Start of Model" and "End of Model."

Without some degree of empirical data (for example, Web server logs from a previous release of the application), target load levels are exactly that—targets. These targets are most frequently set by the business, based on its goals related to the application and whether those goals are market penetration, revenue generation, or something else. These represent the numbers you want to work with at the outset.

Quantifying the Volume of Application Usage

If you have access to Web server logs for a current implementation of the application—whether it is a production implementation of a previous release, a representative prototype, or a beta release—you can use data from these logs to validate and/or enhance the data collected by using the resources above. By performing a quantitative analysis on Web server logs, you can determine:

- The total number of visits to the site over a period of time (month/week/day).
- The volume of usage, in terms of total averages and peak loads, on an hourly basis.
- The duration of sessions for total averages and peak loads on an hourly basis.
- The total hourly averages and peak loads translated into overlapping user sessions to simulate real scalability volume for the load test.
- The business cycles or special events that result in significant changes in usage.

The following are the inputs and outputs used for determining target load levels.

Inputs

- Usage data extracted from Web server logs
- Business volume (both current and projected) mapping to objectives
- Key scenarios
- Distribution of work
- Session characteristics (navigational path, duration, percentage of new users)

Output

By combining the volume information with objectives, key scenarios, user delays, navigation paths, and scenario distributions from the previous steps, you can determine the remaining details necessary to implement the workload model under a particular target load.

Integrating Model Variance

Because the usage models are "best guesses" until production data becomes available, it is a good idea to create no fewer than three usage models for each target load. This has the effect of adding a rough confidence interval to the performance measurements. Stakeholders can focus on the results from one test based on many fallible assumptions, as well as on how many inaccuracies in those assumptions are likely to impact the performance characteristics of the application.

The three usage models that teams generally find most valuable are:

- Anticipated Usage (the model or models you created in the "Determine Individual User Data and Variance" activity)
- Best Case Usage, in terms of performance (that is, weighted heavily in favor of low-performance cost activities)
- Worst Case Usage, in terms of performance (that is, weighted heavily in favor of high-performance cost activities)

The following chart is an example of the information that testing for all three of these models can provide. As you can see, in this particular case the Anticipated Usage and Best Case Usage resulted in similar performance characteristics. However, the Worst Case Usage showed that there is nearly a 50-percent drop-off in the total load that can be supported between it and the Anticipated Usage. Such information could lead to a reevaluation of the usage model, or possibly to a decision to test with the Worst Case Usage model moving forward as a kind of safety factor until empirical data becomes available.

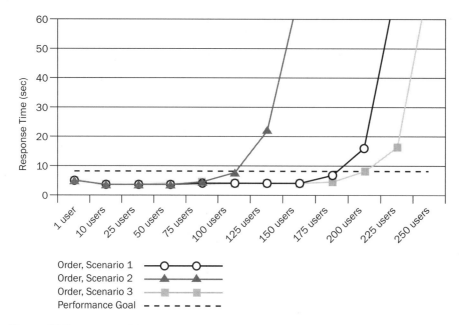

Figure 12.5 *Usage Models*

Considerations

Consider the following key points when identifying target load levels:

- Although the volumes resulting from the activities above may or may not end up correlating to the loads the application will actually encounter, the business will want to know if and how well the application as developed or deployed will support its target loads.

- Because the workload models you have constructed represent the frequency of each activity as a percentage of the total load, you should not need to update your models after determining target load levels.

- Although it frequently is the case that each workload model will be executed at a variety of load levels and that the load level is very easy to change at run time using most load-generation tools, it is still important to identify the expected and peak target load levels for each workload model for the purpose of predicting or comparing with production conditions. Changing load levels even slightly can sometimes change results dramatically.

Prepare to Implement the Model

Implementation of the workload model as an executable test is tightly tied to the implementation method—typically, creating scripts in a load-generation tool. For more information about implementing and validating a test, see Chapter 14, "Test Execution."

Considerations

Consider the following key points when preparing to implement the model:

- Do not change your model without serious consideration simply because the model is difficult to implement in your tool.

- If you cannot implement your model as designed, ensure that you record the details about the model you do implement.

- Implementing the model frequently includes identifying metrics to be collected and determining how to collect those metrics.

Summary

When conducting performance testing with the intent of understanding, predicting, or tuning production performance, it is crucial that test conditions be similar or at least close to production usage or projected future business volume.

For accurate, predictive test results, user behavior must involve modeling the customer sessions based on page flow, frequency of hits, the length of time that users stop between pages, and any other factor specific to how users interact with your Web site.

13

Determining Individual User Data and Variances

Objectives

- Learn how to determine realistic durations and distribution patters for user delay times.
- Learn how to incorporate realistic user delays into test designs and test scripts.
- Learn about key variables to consider when defining workload characterization.
- Learn about the elements of user behavior that will aid with modeling the user experience when creating load tests.

Overview

This chapter describes the process of determining realistic individual user delays, user data, and abandonment. For performance testing to yield results that are directly applicable to understanding the performance characteristics of an application in production, the tested workloads must represent the real-world production environment. To create a reasonably accurate representation of reality, you must model users with a degree variability and randomness similar to that found in a representative cross-section of users.

How to Use This Chapter

Use this chapter to understand how to model variances such as user delays, user data, and user abandonment so that your workload characterization will create realistic usage patterns, thus improving the accuracy of production simulations. To get the most from this chapter:

- Use the "User Delay" section, along with the sections that follow, to understand the key concepts of user delay modeling and its impact on workload characterization.
- Use the "Determining Individual User Data" section to understand the key concepts of user data and its impact on workload characterization.
- Use the "User Abandonment" section to understand the key concepts of user abandonment and its impact on workload characterization.

User Delays

The more accurately users are modeled, the more reliable performance test results will be. One frequently overlooked aspect of accurate user modeling is the modeling of user delays. This section explains how to determine user delay times to be incorporated into your workload model and subsequently into your performance scripts.

During a session, the user can be in a number of different states—browsing, logging onto the system, and so on. Customers will have different modes of interacting with the Web site; some users are familiar with the site and quickly go from one page to another, while others take longer to decide which action they will take. Therefore, characterizing user behavior must involve modeling the customer sessions based on page flow, frequency of hits, the amount of time users' pause between viewing pages, and any other factor specific to how users interact with your Web site.

Consequences of Improperly Modeling User Delays

To ensure realistic load tests, any reasonable attempt at applying ranges and distributions is preferable to ignoring the concept of varying user delays. Creating a load test in which every user spends exactly the same amount of time on each page is simply not realistic and will generate misleading results. For example, you can very easily end up with results similar to the following.

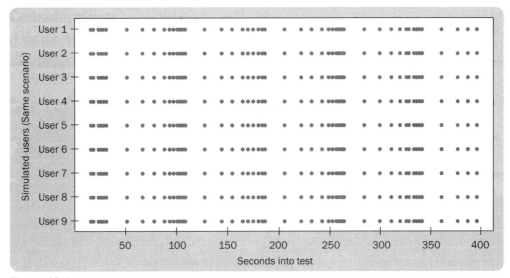

Figure 13.1 *Results for Using Static User Delays*

In case you are not familiar with response graphs, each dot represents a user activity (in this case, a page request); the horizontal axis shows the time, in seconds, from the start of the test run; and individual virtual testers are listed on the vertical axis. This particular response graph is an example of "banding" or "striping." Banding should be avoided when doing load or performance testing, although it may be valuable as a stress test. From the server's perspective, this test is the same as 10 users executing the identical actions synchronously: Home page→ wait x seconds→ page1.

To put a finer point on it, hold a ruler vertically against your screen and move it slowly across the graph from left to right. This is what the server sees: no dots, no dots, no dots, lots of dots, no dots. This is a very poor representation of actual user communities.

The following figure is a much better representation of actual users, achieved by adding some small-range uniform and normally distributed delays to the same test.

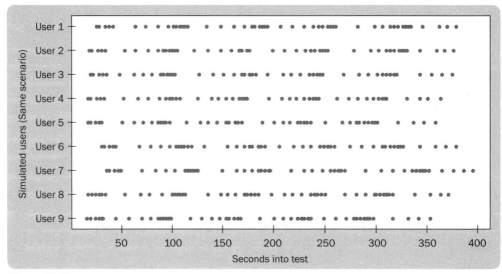

Figure 13.2 *Results for Using Normally Distributed User Delays*

If you perform the same activity with the ruler, you will see that the dots are more evenly distributed this time, which dramatically increases both the realism of the simulated load and the accuracy of the performance test results.

Step 1—Determine User Delays

Delays that occur while users view content on Web pages—also commonly known as *think times*—represent the answers to questions such as "How long does it take a user to enter their login credentials?" and "How much time will users spend reading this page?" You can use several different methods to estimate think times associated with user activities on your Web site. The best method, of course, is to use real data collected about your production site. This is rarely possible, however, because testing generally occurs before the site is released to production. This necessitates making educated guesses or approximations regarding activity on the site.

The most commonly useful methods of determining this include the following:

● When testing a Web site that is already in production, you can determine the actual values and distribution by extracting the average and standard deviation for user viewing (or typing) time from the log file for each page. With this information, you can easily determine the think time for each page. Your production site may also have Web traffic–monitoring software that provides this type of information directly.

- If you have no log files, you can run simple in-house experiments using employees, customers, clients, friends, or family members to determine, for example, the page-viewing time differences between new and returning users. This type of simplified usability study tends to be a highly effective method of data collection for Web sites that have never been live, as well as validation of data collected by using other methods.

- Time yourself using the site, or by performing similar actions on a similar site. Obviously, this method is highly vulnerable to personal bias, but it is a reasonable place to start until you get a chance to time actual users during User Acceptance Testing (UAT) or conduct your own usability study.

- In the absence of any better source of information, you can leverage some of the metrics and statistics that have already been collected by research companies such as Nielsen//NetRatings, Keynote, or MediaMetrix. These statistics provide data on average page-viewing times and user session duration based on an impersonal sample of users and Web sites. Although these numbers are not from your specific Web site, they can work quite well as first approximations.

There is no need to spend a lot of time collecting statistically significant volumes of data, or to be excessively precise. All you really need to know is how long a typical user will spend performing an activity, give or take a second or two. However, depending on the nature of your site, you may want to determine user delay times separately for first-time and experienced users.

Step 2—Apply Delay Ranges

Simply determining how much time one person spends visiting your pages, or what the variance in time between users is, is not enough in itself—you must vary delay times by user. It is extremely unlikely that each user will spend exactly the same amount of time on a page. It is also extremely likely that conducting a performance test in which all users spend the same amount of time on a page will lead to unrealistic or at least unreliable results.

To convert the delay times or delay ranges from step 1 into something that also represents the variability between users, the following three pieces of information are required:

- The minimum delay time
- The maximum delay time
- The distribution or pattern of user delays between those points

If you do not have a minimum and maximum value from your analysis in step 1, you can apply heuristics as follows to determine acceptable estimates:

- The minimum value could be:
  - An experienced user who intended to go to the page but will not remain there long (for example, a user who only needs the page to load in order to scan, find, and click the next link).
  - A user who realized that they clicked to the wrong page.
  - A user who clicked through a form that had all of its values pre-filled.
  - The minimum length of time you think a user needs to type the required information into the form.
  - Half of the value that you determined was "typical."
- The maximum value could be:
  - Session time-out.
  - Sufficient time for a user to look up information for a form.
  - No longer than it takes a slow reader to read the entire page.
  - The time it takes to read, three times out loud, the text that users are expected to read. (This is the heuristic used by the film industry for any onscreen text.)
  - Double the value that you determined was "typical."

Although you want your estimate to be relatively close to reality, any range that covers ~75 percent of the expected users is sufficient to ensure that you are not unintentionally skewing your results.

Step 3—Apply Distributions

There are numerous mathematical models for these types of distributions. Four of these models cover the overwhelming majority of user delay scenarios:

- Linear or uniform distribution
- Normal distribution
- Negative exponential distribution
- Double hump normal distribution

Linear or Uniform Distribution

A uniform distribution between a minimum and a maximum value is the easiest to model. This distribution model simply selects random numbers that are evenly distributed between the upper and lower bounds of the range. This means that it is no more likely that the number generated will be closer to the middle or either end of the range. The figure below shows a uniform distribution of 1000 values generated between 0 and 25. Use a uniform distribution in situations where there is a reasonably clear minimum and maximum value, but either have or expect to have a distinguishable pattern between those end points.

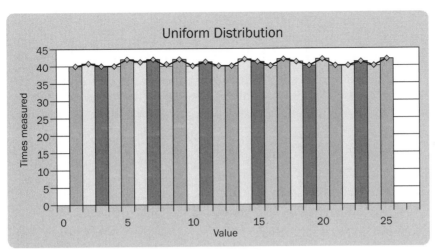

Figure 13.3 *Uniform Distribution*

Normal Distribution

A normal distribution, also known as a *bell curve*, is more difficult to model but is more accurate in almost all cases. This distribution model selects numbers randomly in such a way that the frequency of selection is weighted toward the center, or average value. The figure below shows a normal distribution of 1000 values generated between 0 and 25 (that is, a mean of 12.5 and a standard deviation of 3.2). Normal distribution is generally considered to be the most accurate mathematical model of quantifiable measures of large cross-sections of people when actual data is unavailable. Use a normal distribution in any situation where you expect the pattern to be shifted toward the center of the end points. The valid range of values for the standard deviation is from 0 (equivalent to a static delay of the midpoint between the maximum and minimum values) and the maximum value minus the minimum value (equivalent to a uniform distribution). If you have no way to determine the actual standard deviation, a reasonable approximation is 25 percent of (or .25 times the range) of the delay.

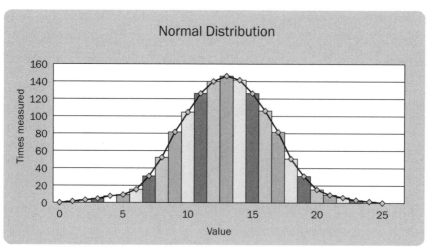

Figure 13.4 *Normal Distribution*

Negative Exponential Distribution

Negative exponential distribution creates a distribution similar to that shown in the graph below. This model skews the frequency of delay times strongly toward one end of the range. This model is most useful for situations such as users clicking a "play again" link that only activates after multimedia content has completed playing. The following figure shows a negative exponential distribution of 1000 values generated between 0 and 25.

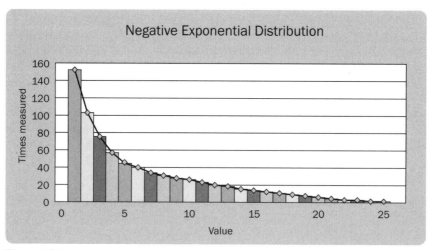

Figure 13.5 *Negative Exponential Distribution*

Double Hump Normal Distribution

The double hump normal distribution creates a distribution similar to that shown in the graph below. To understand when this distribution would be used, consider the first time you visit a Web page that has a large amount of text. On that first visit, you will probably want to read the text, but the next time you might simply click through that page on the way to a page located deeper in the site. This is precisely the type of user behavior this distribution represents. The figure below shows that 60 percent of the users who view this page spend about 8 seconds on the page scanning for the next link to click, and the other 40 percent of the users actually read the entire page, which takes about 45 seconds. You can see that both humps are normal distributions with different minimum, maximum, and standard deviation values.

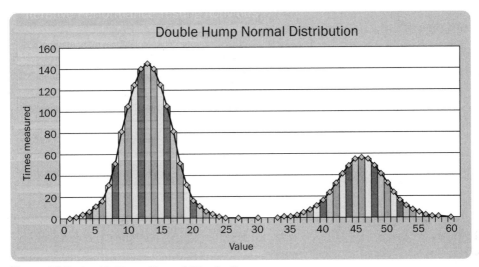

Figure 13.6 *Double Hump Normal Distribution*

To implement this pattern, simply write a snippet of code to generate a number between 1 and 100 to represent a percentage of users. If that number is below a certain threshold (in the graph above, below 61), call the normal distribution function with the parameters to generate delays with the first distribution pattern. If that number is at or above that threshold, call the normal distribution function with the correct parameters to generate the second distribution pattern.

Determining Individual User Data

Once you have a list of key scenarios, you will need to determine how individual users actually accomplish the tasks or activities related to those scenarios, and the user-specific data associated with a user accomplishing that task or activity.

Unfortunately, navigation paths alone do not provide all of the information required to implement a workload simulation. To fully implement the workload model, you need several more pieces of information. This information includes:

- How long users may spend on a page?
- What data may need to be entered on each page?
- What conditions may cause a user to change navigation paths?

Considerations

Consider the following key points when identifying unique data for navigation paths and/or simulated users:

- Performance tests frequently consume large amounts of test data. Ensure that you have enough data to conduct an effective test.
- Using the same data repeatedly will frequently lead to invalid performance test results.
- Especially when designing and debugging performance tests, test databases can become dramatically overloaded with data. Periodically check to see if the data base is storing unrealistic volumes of data for the situation you are trying to simulate.
- Consider including invalid data in your performance tests. For example, include some users who mistype their password on the first attempt but do it correctly on a second try.
- First-time users usually spend significantly longer on each page or activity than experienced users.
- The best possible test data is test data collected from a production database or log file.
- Consider client-side caching. First-time users will be downloading every object on the site, while frequent visitors are likely to have many static objects and/or cookies stored in their local cache. When capturing the uniqueness of the user's behavior, consider whether that user represents a first-time user or a user with an established client-side cache.

User Abandonment

User abandonment refers to situations where customers exit the Web site before completing a task, because of performance slowness. People have different rates of tolerance for performance, depending on their psychological profile and the type of page they request. Failing to account for user abandonment will cause loads that are highly unrealistic and improbable. Load tests should simulate user abandonment as realistically as possible or they may cause types of load that will never occur in real life—and create bottlenecks that might never happen with real users. Load tests should report the number of users that might abandon the Web site due to poor performance.

In a typical Web site traffic pattern, when the load gets too heavy for the system/ application to handle, the site slows down, causing people to abandon it, thus decreasing the load until the system speeds back up to an acceptable rate. Abandonment creates a self-policing mechanism that recovers performance at previous levels (when the overload occurred), even at the cost of losing some customers. Therefore, one reason to accurately account for user abandonment is to see just how many users "some" is. Another reason is to determine the actual volume your application can maintain before you start losing customers. Yet another reason to account for user abandonment is to avoid simulating, and subsequently resolving, bottlenecks that realistically might not even be possible.

If you do not account for abandonment at all, the load test may wait indefinitely to receive the page or object it requested. When the test eventually receives that object, even if "eventually" takes hours longer than a real user would wait, the test will move on to the next object as if nothing were wrong. If the request for an object simply is not acknowledged, the test skips it and makes a note in the test execution log with no regard as to whether that object was critical to the user. Note that there *are* some cases where not accounting for abandonment is an accurate representation of reality; for instance, a Web-based application that has been exclusively created for an audience that has no choice but to wait because there are no alternative methods of completing a required task.

Considerations

The following are generally useful guidelines related to user abandonment:

- Check the abandonment rate before evaluating response times. If the abandonment rate for a particular page is less than about 2 percent, consider the possibility of those response times being outliers.

- Check the abandonment rate before drawing conclusions about load. Remember, every user who abandons is one less user applying load. Although the response-time statistics may look good, if you have 75-percent abandonment, load is roughly 75 percent lighter than it was being tested for.

- If the abandonment rate is more than about 20 percent, consider disabling the abandonment routine and re-executing the test to help gain information about what is causing the problem.

Summary

The process of designing realistic user delays into tests and test scripts is critical for workload characterizations to generate accurate results. For performance testing to yield results that are directly applicable to understanding the performance charac-teristics of an application in production or a projected future business volume, the tested workloads must represent reality, replicating user delay patterns.

To create a reasonably accurate representation of reality, you must model user delays with variability and randomness by taking into account individual user data and user abandonment, similar to a representative cross-section of users.

Part VI
Execute Tests

In this part:

- Test Execution

14

Test Execution

Objectives

- Understand common principles and considerations of performance test execution.
- Understand the common activities of performance test execution.

Overview

Performance test execution is the activity that occurs between developing test scripts and reporting and analyzing test results. Much of the performance testing–related training available today treats this activity as little more than starting a test and monitoring it to ensure that the test appears to be running as expected. In reality, this activity is significantly more complex than just clicking a button and monitoring machines. This chapter addresses these complexities based on numerous real-world project experiences.

How to Use this Chapter

Use this chapter to understand the key principles and considerations underlying performance test execution and the various activities that it entails. To get the most from this chapter:

- Use the "Approach for Test Execution" section to get an overview of the approach for performance test execution and as quick reference guide for you and your team.
- Use the various activity sections to understand the details of each activity involved in performance test execution.

Approach for Test Execution

The following activities are involved in performance test execution:

- Validate the test environment
- Validate tests
- Run tests
- Baseline and benchmark
- Archive tests

The following sections discuss each of these activities in detail.

Validate the Test Environment

The goal is for the test environment to mirror your production environment as closely as possible. Typically, any differences between the test and production environments are noted and accounted for while designing tests. Before running your tests, it is important to validate that the test environment matches the configuration that you were expecting and/or designed your test for. If the test environment is even slightly different from the environment you designed your tests to be run against, there is a high probability that your tests might not work at all, or worse, that they will work but will provide misleading data.

The following activities frequently prove valuable when validating a test environment:

- Ensure that the test environment is correctly configured for metrics collection.
- Turn off any active virus-scanning on load-generating machines during testing, to minimize the likelihood of unintentionally skewing results data as a side-effect of resource consumption by the antivirus/anti-spyware software.
- Consider simulating background activity, when necessary. For example, many servers run batch processing during predetermined time periods, while servicing users' requests. Not accounting for such activities in those periods may result in overly optimistic performance results.
- Run simple usage scenarios to validate the Web server layer first if possible, separately from other layers. Run your scripts without think times. Try to run a scenario that does not include database activity. Inability to utilize 100 percent of the Web server's processor can indicate a network problem or that the load generator clients have reached their maximum output capacity.
- Run simple usage scenarios that are limited to reading data to validate database scenarios. Run your script without think times. Use test data feeds to simulate randomness. For example, query for a set of products. Inability to utilize 100 percent of the Web server's processor can indicate a network problem or that the load-generator clients have reached their maximum output capacity.

- Validate the test environment by running more complex usage scenarios with updates and writes to the database, using a mix of test scripts that simulate business actions.

- In Web farm environments, check to see if your load tests are implementing Internet Protocol (IP) switching. Not doing so may cause IP affinity, a situation where all of the requests from the load-generation client machine are routed to the same server rather than being balanced across all of the servers in the farm. IP affinity leads to inaccurate load test results because other servers participating in the load balancing will not be utilized.

- Work with key performance indicators (KPIs) on all the servers to assess your test environment (processor, network, disk, and memory). Include all servers in the cluster to ensure correct evaluation of your environment.

- Consider spending time creating data feeds for the test application. For example, database tables containing production data such as number of users, products, and orders shipped, so that you can create similar conditions to replicate problems in critical usage scenarios. Many scenarios involve running queries against tables containing several thousands of entries, to simulate lock timeouts or deadlocks.

Additional Considerations

Consider the following key points when troubleshooting performance-testing environments:

- Look for problems in the load-generation clients from which load is simulated. Client machines often produce inaccurate performance-testing results due to insufficient processor or memory resources. Consider adding more client computers to compensate for fast transactions that may cause higher processor utilization; also consider using more memory when this becomes the bottleneck. Memory can be consumed when test data feeds are cached in load generators, or by more complex scripting in load tests.

- Some network interface cards (NICs) when set to auto mode will fail to negotiate with switches in proper full-duplex mode. The result is that the NICs will operate in half-duplex negotiation, which causes inaccurate performance-testing results. A typical perimeter network with a Web server and database server in different layers will be deployed with the Web server having two NICs, one facing your clients and another using a different route to communicate with the database layer. However, be aware that having one NIC in the Web server facing both the clients and the database tier may cause network bottleneck congestion.

- The database server in the production environment may be using separate hard drives for log files and data files associated with the database as a matter of policy. Replicate such deployment configurations to avoid inaccurate performance-testing results. Consider that if DNS is not properly configured, it might cause broadcast messages to be sent when opening database connections by using the database server name. Name-resolution issues may cause connections to open slowly.

- Improper data feeds consumed by your scripts will frequently cause you to overlook problems with the environment. For example, low processor activity may be caused by artificial locking due to scripts querying the same record from the database. Consider creating test data feeds that simulate the correct business actions, accounting for variability of data sent from the post request. Load-generation tools may use a central repository such as a database or files in a directory structure to collect performance test data. Make sure that the data repository is located on a machine that will not cause traffic in the route used by your load-generation tools; for example, putting the data repository in the same virtual local-area network (VLAN) of the machine used to manage data collection.

- Load-generation tools may require the use of special accounts between load-generator machines and the computers that collect performance data. Make sure that you set such configurations correctly. Verify that data collection is occurring in the test environment, taking into consideration that the traffic may be required to pass through a firewall.

Validate Tests

Poor load simulations can render all previous work useless. To understand the data collected from a test run, the load simulation must accurately reflect the test design. When the simulation does not reflect the test design, the results are prone to misinterpretation. Even if your tests accurately reflect the test design, there are still many ways that the test can yield invalid or misleading results. Although it may be tempting to simply trust your tests, it is almost always worth the time and effort to validate the accuracy of your tests before you need to depend on them to provide results intended to assist in making the "go-live" decision. It may be useful to think about test validation in terms of the following four categories:

- **Test design implementation.** To validate that you have implemented your test design accurately (using whatever method you have chosen), you will need to run the test and examine exactly what the test does.

- **Concurrency.** After you have validated that your test conforms to the test design when run with a single user, run the test with several users. Ensure that each user is seeded with unique data, and that users begin their activity within a few seconds of one another — not all at the same second, as this is likely to create an unrealistically stressful situation that would add complexity to validating the accuracy of your test design implementation. One method of validating that tests run as expected with multiple users is to use three test runs; one with 3 users, one with 5 users, and one with 11 users. These three tests have a tendency to expose many common issues with both the configuration of the test environment (such as a limited license being installed on an application component) and the test itself (such as parameterized data not varying as intended).

- **Combinations of tests.** Having validated that a test runs as intended with a single user and with multiple users, the next logical step is to validate that the test runs accurately in combination with other tests. Generally, when testing performance, tests get mixed and matched to represent various combinations and distributions of users, activities, and scenarios. If you do not validate that your tests have been both designed and implemented to handle this degree of complexity prior to running critical test projects, you can end up wasting a lot of time debugging your tests or test scripts when you could have been collecting valuable performance information.

- **Test data validation.** Once you are satisfied that your tests are running properly, the last critical validation step is to validate your test data. Performance testing can utilize and/or consume large volumes of test data, thereby increasing the likelihood of errors in your dataset. In addition to the data used by your tests, it is important to validate that your tests share that data as intended, and that the application under test is seeded with the correct data to enable your tests.

Dynamic Data

The following are technical reasons for using dynamic data correctly in load test scripts:

- Using the same data value causes artificial usage of caching because the system will retrieve data from copies in memory. This can happen throughout different layers and components of the system, including databases, file caches of the operating systems, hard drives, storage controllers, and buffer managers. Reusing data from the cache during performance testing might account for faster testing results than would occur in the real world.

- Some business scenarios require a relatively small range of data selection. In such a case, even reusing the cache more frequently will simulate other performance-related problems, such as database deadlocks and slower response times due to timeouts caused by queries to the same items. This type of scenario is typical of marketing campaigns and seasonal sales events.

- Some business scenarios require using unique data during load testing; for example, if the server returns session-specific identifiers during a session after login to the site with a specific set of credentials. Reusing the same login data would cause the server to return a bad session identifier error. Another frequent scenario is when the user enters a unique set of data, or the system fails to accept the selection; for example, registering new users that would require entering a unique user ID on the registration page.

- In some business scenarios, you need to control the number of parameterized items; for example, a caching component that needs to be tested for its memory footprint to evaluate server capacity, with a varying number of products in the cache.

- In some business scenarios, you need to reduce the script size or the number of scripts; for example, several instances of an application will live in one server, reproducing a scenario where an independent software vendor (ISV) will host them. In this scenario, the Uniform Resource Locators (URLs) need to be parameterized during load test execution for the same business scenarios.

- Using dynamic test data in a load test tends to reproduce more complicated and time-sensitive bugs; for example, a deadlock encountered as a result of performing different actions using different user accounts.

- Using dynamic test data in a load test allows you to use error values if they suit your test plan; for example, using an ID that is always a positive number when testing to simulate hacker behavior. It may be beneficial to use zero or negative values when testing to replicate application errors, such as scanning the database table when an invalid value is supplied.

Test Validation

The following are some commonly employed methods of test validation, which are frequently used in combination with one another:

- Run the test first with a single user only. This makes initial validation much less complex.

- Observe your test while it is running and pay close attention to any behavior you feel is unusual. Your instincts are usually right, or at least valuable.

- Use the system manually during test execution so that you can compare your observations with the results data at a later time.

- Make sure that the test results and collected metrics represent what you intended them to represent.

- Check to see if any of the parent requests or dependent requests failed.

- Check the content of the returned pages, as load-generation tools sometimes report summary results that appear to "pass" even though the correct page or data was not returned.

- Run a test that loops through all of your data to check for unexpected errors.

- If appropriate, validate that you can reset test and/or application data following a test run.

- At the conclusion of your test run, check the application database to ensure that it has been updated (or not) according to your test design. Consider that many transactions in which the Web server returns a success status with a "200" code might be failing internally; for example, errors due to a previously used user name in a new user registration scenario, or an order number that is already in use.

- Consider cleaning the database entries between error trials to eliminate data that might be causing test failures; for example, order entries that you cannot reuse in subsequent test execution.
- Run tests in a variety of combinations and sequences to ensure that one test does not corrupt data needed by another test in order to run properly.

Additional Considerations

Consider the following additional points when validating your tests:

- Do not use performance results data from your validation test runs as part of your final report.
- Report performance issues uncovered during your validation test runs.
- Use appropriate load-generation tools to create a load that has the characteristics specified in your test design.
- Ensure that the intended performance counters for identified metrics and resource utilization are being measured and recorded, and that they are not interfering with the accuracy of the simulation.
- Run other tests during your performance test to ensure that the simulation is not impacting other parts of the system. These other tests may be either automated or manual.
- Repeat your test, adjusting variables such as user names and think times to see if the test continues to behave as anticipated.
- Remember to simulate ramp-up and cool-down periods appropriately.

Questions to Ask

- What additional team members should be involved in evaluating the accuracy of this test?
- Do the preliminary results make sense?
- Is the test providing the data we expected?

Run Tests

Although the process and flow of running tests are extremely dependent on your tools, environment, and project context, there are some fairly universal tasks and considerations to keep in mind when running tests.

Once it has been determined that the application under test is in an appropriate state to have performance tests run against it, the testing generally begins with the highest-priority performance test that can reasonably be completed based on the current state of the project and application. After each test run, compile a brief summary of what happened during the test and add these comments to the test log for future reference. These comments may address machine failures, application exceptions and errors, network problems, or exhausted disk space or logs. After completing the final test run, ensure that you have saved all of the test results and performance logs before you dismantle the test environment.

Whenever possible, limit tasks to one to two days each to ensure that no time will be lost if the results from a particular test or battery of tests turn out to be inconclusive, or if the initial test design needs modification to produce the intended results. One of the most important tasks when running tests is to remember to modify the tests, test designs, and subsequent strategies as results analysis leads to new priorities.

A widely recommended guiding principle is: *Run test tasks in one- to two-day batches. See the tasks through to completion, but be willing to take important detours along the way if an opportunity to add additional value presents itself.*

Keys to Efficiently and Effectively Running Tests

In general, the keys to efficiently and effectively running tests include:

- Revisit performance-testing priorities after no more than two days.
- Remember to capture and use a performance baseline.
- Plan to spend some time fixing application errors, or debugging the test.
- Analyze results immediately so that you can modify your test plan accordingly.
- Communicate test results frequently and openly across the team.
- Record results and significant findings.
- Record other data needed to repeat the test later.
- At appropriate points during test execution, stress the application to its maximum capacity or user load, as this can provide extremely valuable information.
- Remember to validate application tuning or optimizations.
- Consider evaluating the effect of application failover and recovery.
- Consider measuring the effects of different system configurations.

Additional Considerations

Consider the following additional points when running your tests:

- Performance testing is frequently conducted on an isolated network segment to prevent disruption of other business operations. If this is not the case for your test project, ensure that you obtain permission to generate loads during certain hours on the available network.

- Before running the real test, consider executing a quick "smoke test" to make sure that the test script and remote performance counters are working correctly.

- If you choose to execute a smoke test, do not report the results as official or formal parts of your testing.

- Reset the system (unless your scenario is to do otherwise) before running a formal test.

- If at all possible, execute every test twice. If the results produced are not very similar, execute the test again. Try to determine what factors account for the difference.

- No matter how far in advance a test is scheduled, give the team 30-minute and 5-minute warnings before launching the test (or starting the day's testing). Inform the team whenever you are not going to be executing for more than one hour in succession.

- Do not process data, write reports, or draw diagrams on your load-generating machine while generating a load because this can corrupt the data.

- Do not throw away the first iteration because of script compilation or other reasons. Instead, measure this iteration separately so you will know what the first user after a system-wide reboot can expect.

- Test execution is never really finished, but eventually you will reach a point of diminishing returns on a particular test. When you stop obtaining valuable information, change your test.

- If neither you nor your development team can figure out the cause of an issue in twice as much time as it took the test to execute, it may be more efficient to eliminate one or more variables/potential causes and try again.

- If your intent is to measure performance related to a particular load, it is important to allow time for the system to stabilize between increases in load to ensure the accuracy of measurements.

- Make sure that the client computers (also known as load-generation client machines) that you use to generate load are not overly stressed. Utilization of resources such as processor and memory should remain low enough to ensure that the load-generation environment is not itself a bottleneck.

- Analyze results immediately and modify your test plan accordingly.

- Work closely with the team or team sub-set that is most relevant to the test.

- Communicate test results frequently and openly across the team.

- If you will be repeating the test, consider establishing a test data restore point before you begin testing.

- In most cases, maintaining a test execution log that captures notes and observations for each run is invaluable.

- Treat workload characterization as a moving target. Adjust new settings for think times and number of users to model the new total number of users for normal and peak loads.

- Observe your test during execution and pay close attention to any behavior you feel is unusual. Your instincts are usually right, or at least valuable.

- Ensure that performance counters relevant for identified metrics and resource utilization are being measured and are not interfering with the accuracy of the simulation.

- Use the system manually during test execution so that you can compare your observations with the results data at a later time.

- Remember to simulate ramp-up and cool-down periods appropriately.

Questions to Ask:

- Have recent test results or project updates made this task more or less valuable compared to other tests we could be conducting right now?

- What additional team members should be involved with this task?

- Do the preliminary results make sense?

Baseline and Benchmark

When baselines and benchmarks are used, they are generally the first and last tests you will execute, respectively. Of all the tests that may be executed during the course of a project, it is most important that baselines and benchmarks be well understood and controlled, making the validations discussed above even more important.

Baselines

Creating a *baseline* is the process of running a set of tests to capture performance metric data for the purpose of evaluating the effectiveness of subsequent performance-improving changes to the system or application.

With respect to Web applications, you can use a baseline to determine whether performance is improving or declining and to find deviations across builds and versions. For example, you could measure load time, number of transactions processed per unit of time, number of Web pages served per unit of time, and resource utilization such as memory and processor usage. Some considerations about using baselines include:

- A baseline can be created for a system, component, or application.

- A baseline can be created at different layers: database, Web services, etc.

- A baseline can be used as a standard for comparison to track future optimizations or regressions. When using a baseline for this purpose, it is important to validate that the baseline tests and results are well understood and repeatable.

- Baselines can help product teams articulate variances that represent degradation or optimization during the course of the development life cycle by providing a known starting point for trend analysis. Baselines are most valuable if created using a set of reusable test assets; it is important that such tests are representative of workload characteristics that are both repeatable and provide an appropriately accurate simulation.

- Baseline results can be articulated by using combinations of a broad set of key performance indicators such as response time, processor, memory, disk, and network.

- Sharing baseline results across the team establishes a common foundation of information about performance characteristics to enable future communication about performance changes in an application or component.

- A baseline is specific to an application and is most useful for comparing performance across different builds, versions, or releases.

- Establishing a baseline before making configuration changes almost always saves time because it enables you to quickly determine what effect the changes had on the application's performance.

Benchmarking

Benchmarking is the process of comparing your system performance against an industry standard that is endorsed by some other organization.

From the perspective of Web application development, benchmarking involves running a set of tests that comply with the specifications of an industry benchmark to capture the performance metrics for your application necessary to determine its benchmark score. You can then compare your application against other systems or applications that have also calculated their score for the same benchmark. You may choose to tune your application performance to achieve or surpass a certain benchmark score. Some considerations about benchmarking include:

- A benchmark score is achieved by working within industry specifications or by porting an existing implementation to comply with those specifications.

- Benchmarking generally requires identifying all of the necessary components that will run together, the market where the product exists, and the specific metrics to measure.

- Benchmark scores can be published publicly and may result in comparisons being made by competitors. Performance metrics that may be included along with benchmark scores include response time, transactions processed per unit of time, Web pages accessed per unit of time, processor usage, memory usage, and search times.

Archive Tests

Some degree of change control or version control can be extremely valuable for managing scripts, scenarios, and/or data changes between each test execution, and for communicating these differences to the rest of the team. Some teams prefer to check their test scripts, results, and reports into the same version-control system as the build of the application to which they apply. Other teams simply save copies into dated folders on a periodic basis, or have their own version-control software dedicated to the performance team. It is up to you and your team to decide what method is going to work best for you, but in most cases archiving tests, test data, and test results saves much more time than it takes over the course of a performance-testing project.

Additional Considerations

Consider the following additional points when creating baselines and benchmarking:

- You can use archived test scripts, data, and results to create the baseline for the next version of your product. Archiving this information together with the build of the software that was tested satisfies many auditability standards.

- In most cases, performance test scripts are improved or modified with each new build. If you do not save a copy of the script and identify the build it was used against, you can end up doing a lot of extra work to get your scripts running again in the case of a build rollback.

- With the overwhelming majority of load-generation tools, implementing the test is a minor software-development effort in itself. While this effort generally does not need to follow all of the team's standards and procedures for software development, it is a good idea to adopt a sound and appropriately "weighted" development process for performance scripts that complements or parallels the process your development team employs.

Summary

Performance test execution involves activities such as validating test environments/scripts, running the test, and generating the test results. It can also include creating baselines and/or benchmarks of the performance characteristics.

It is important to validate the test environment to ensure that the environment truly represents the production environment.

Validate test scripts to check if correct metrics are being collected, and if the test script design is correctly simulating workload characteristics.

Part VII
Analyze Results and Report

In this part:

- Key Mathematic Principles for Performance Testers
- Performance Test Reporting Fundamentals

15

Key Mathematic Principles for Performance Testers

Objectives

- Learn the uses, meanings of, and concepts underlying common mathematical and statistical principles as they apply to performance test analysis and reporting.

Overview

Members of software development teams, developers, testers, administrators, and managers alike need to know how to apply mathematics and interpret statistical data in order to do their jobs effectively. Performance analysis and reporting are particularly math-intensive. This chapter describes the most commonly used, mis-applied, and misunderstood mathematical and statistical concepts in performance testing, in a way that will benefit any member of the team.

Even though there is a need to understand many mathematical and statistical concepts, many software developers, testers, and managers either do not have strong backgrounds in or do not enjoy mathematics and statistics. This leads to significant misrepresentations and misinterpretation of performance-testing results. The information presented in this article is not intended to replace formal training in these areas, but rather to provide common language and commonsense explanations for mathematical and statistical operations that are valuable to understanding performance testing.

How to Use This Chapter

Use this chapter to understand the different metrics and calculations that are used for analyzing performance data results and preparing performance results reports. To get the most from this chapter:

- Use the "Exemplar Data Sets" section to gain an understanding of the exemplars, which are used to illustrate the key mathematical principles explained throughout the chapter.

- Use the remaining sections to learn about key mathematical principles that will help you to understand and present meaningful performance testing reports.

Exemplar Data Sets

This chapter refers to three exemplar data sets for the purposes of illustration, namely.

- Data Set A
- Data Set B
- Data Set C

Data Sets Summary

The following is a summary of Data Sets A, B, and C.

	Sample Size	Minimum	Maximum	Average	Median	Normal	Mode	95th Percentile	Standard Deviation
Data Set A	100	1	7	4	4	4	4	6	1.5
Data Set B	100	1	16	4	1	3	1	16	6.0
Data Set C	100	0	8	4	4	1	3	8	2.6

Figure 15.1 *Summary of Data Sets A, B, and C*

Data Set A

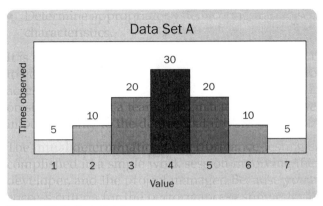

Figure 15.2 *Data Set A*

100 total data points, distributed as follows:

- 5 data points have a value of 1.
- 10 data points have a value of 2.
- 20 data points have a value of 3.
- 30 data points have a value of 4.
- 20 data points have a value of 5.
- 10 data points have a value of 6.
- 5 data points have a value of 7.

Data Set B

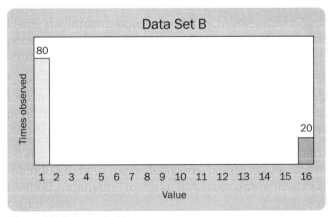

Figure 15.3 *Data Set B*

100 total data points, distributed as follows:

- 80 data points have a value of 1.
- 20 data points have a value of 16.

Data Set C

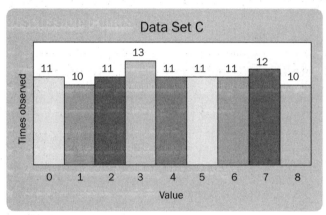

Figure 15.4 *Data Set C*

100 total data points, distributed as follows:

- 11 data points have a value of 0.
- 10 data points have a value of 1.
- 11 data points have a value of 2.
- 13 data points have a value of 3.
- 11 data points have a value of 4.
- 11 data points have a value of 5.
- 11 data points have a value of 6.
- 12 data points have a value of 7.
- 10 data points have a value of 8.

Averages

An average—also known as an *arithmetic mean*, or *mean* for short—is probably the most commonly used, and most commonly misunderstood, statistic of all. To calculate an average, you simply add up all the numbers and divide the sum by the quantity of numbers you just added. What seems to confound many people the most when it comes to performance testing is that, in this example, Data Sets A, B, and C each have an average of exactly 4. In terms of application response times, these sets of data have extremely different meanings. Given a response time goal of 5 seconds, looking at only the average of these sets, all three seem to meet the goal. Looking at the data, however, shows that none of the data sets is composed only of data that meets the goal, and that Data Set B probably demonstrates some kind of performance anomaly. Use caution when using averages to discuss response times and, if at all possible, avoid using averages as the only reported statistic. When reporting averages, it is a good idea to include the sample size, minimum value, maximum value, and standard deviation for the data set.

Percentiles

Few people involved with developing software are familiar with percentiles. A *percentile* is a straightforward concept that is easier to demonstrate than define. For example, to find the 95th percentile value for a data set consisting of 100 page-response-time measurements, you would sort the measurements from largest to smallest and then count down six data points from the largest. The 6th data point value represents the 95th percentile of those measurements. For the purposes of response times, this statistic is read "95 percent of the simulated users experienced a response time of [the 6th-slowest value] or less for this test scenario."

It is important to note that percentile statistics can only stand alone when used to represent data that is uniformly or normally distributed with an acceptable number of outliers (see "Statistical Outliers" below). To illustrate this point, consider the exemplar data sets. The 95th percentile of Data Set B is 16 seconds. Obviously, this does not give the impression of achieving the 5-second response time goal. Interestingly, this can be misleading as well because the 80th percentile value of Data Set B is 1 second. With a response time goal of 5 seconds, it is likely unacceptable to have any response times of 16 seconds, so in this case neither of these percentile values represent the data in a manner that is useful to summarizing response time.

Data Set A is a normally distributed data set that has a 95th percentile value of 6 seconds, an 85th percentile value of 5 seconds, and a maximum value of 7 seconds. In this case, reporting either the 85th or 95th percentile values represents the data in a manner where the assumptions a stakeholder is likely to make about the data are likely to be appropriate to the data.

Medians

A *median* is simply the middle value in a data set when sequenced from lowest to highest. In cases where there is an even number of data points and the two center values are not the same, some disciplines suggest that the median is the average of the two center data points, while others suggest choosing the value closer to the average of the entire set of data. In the case of the exemplar data sets, Data Sets A and B have median values of 4, and Data Set C has a median value of 1.

Normal Values

A *normal value* is the single value that occurs most often in a data set. Data Set A has a normal value of 4, Data Set B has a normal value of 3, and Data Set C has a normal value of 1.

Standard Deviations

By definition, one *standard deviation* is the amount of variance within a set of measurements that encompasses approximately the top 68 percent of all measurements in the data set; in other words, knowing the standard deviation of your data set tells you how densely the data points are clustered around the mean. Simply put, the smaller the standard deviation, the more consistent the data. To illustrate, the standard deviation of Data Set A is approximately 1.5, the standard deviation of Data Set B is approximately 6.0, and the standard deviation of Data Set C is approximately 2.6.

A common rule in this case is: "Data with a standard deviation greater than half of its mean should be treated as suspect. If the data is accurate, the phenomenon the data represents is not displaying a normal distribution pattern." Applying this rule, Data Set A is likely to be a reasonable example of a normal distribution; Data Set B may or may not be a reasonable representation of a normal distribution; and Data Set C is undoubtedly not a reasonable representation of a normal distribution.

Uniform Distributions

Uniform distributions—sometimes known as *linear distributions*—represent a collection of data that is roughly equivalent to a set of random numbers evenly spaced between the upper and lower bounds. In a uniform distribution, every number in the data set is represented approximately the same number of times. Uniform distributions are frequently used when modeling user delays, but are not common in response time results data. In fact, uniformly distributed results in response time data may be an indication of suspect results.

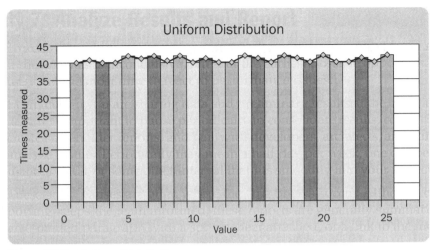

Figure 15.5 *Uniform Distributions*

Normal Distributions

Also known as *bell curves*, *normal distributions* are data sets whose member data are weighted toward the center (or median value). When graphed, the shape of the "bell" of normally distributed data can vary from tall and narrow to short and squat, depending on the standard deviation of the data set. The smaller the standard deviation, the taller and more narrow the "bell." Statistically speaking, most measurements of human variance result in data sets that are normally distributed. As it turns out, end-user response times for Web applications are also frequently normally distributed.

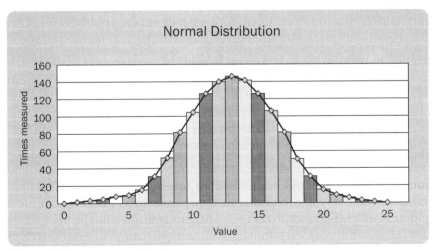

Figure 15.6 *Normal Distribution*

Statistical Significance

Mathematically calculating statistical significance, or reliability, based on sample size is a task that is too arduous and complex for most commercially driven software-development projects. Fortunately, there is a commonsense approach that is both efficient and accurate enough to identify the most significant concerns related to statistical significance. Unless you have a good reason to use a mathematically rigorous calculation for statistical significance, a commonsense approximation is generally sufficient. In support of the commonsense approach described below, consider this excerpt from a StatSoft, Inc. (*http://www.statsoftinc.com*) discussion on the topic:

There is no way to avoid arbitrariness in the final decision as to what level of significance will be treated as really 'significant.' That is, the selection of some level of significance, up to which the results will be rejected as invalid, is arbitrary.

Typically, it is fairly easy to add iterations to performance tests to increase the total number of measurements collected; the best way to ensure statistical significance is simply to collect additional data if there is any doubt about whether or not the collected data represents reality. Whenever possible, ensure that you obtain a sample size of at least 100 measurements from at least two independent tests.

Although there is no strict rule about how to decide which results are statistically similar without complex equations that call for huge volumes of data that commercially driven software projects rarely have the time or resources to collect, the following is a reasonable approach to apply if there is doubt about the significance or reliability of data after evaluating two test executions where the data was expected to be similar. Compare results from at least five test executions and apply the rules of thumb below to determine whether or not test results are similar enough to be considered reliable:

If more than 20 percent (or one out of five) of the test-execution results appear not to be similar to the others, something is generally wrong with the test environment, the application, or the test itself.

1. If a 90th percentile value for any test execution is greater than the maximum or less than the minimum value for any of the other test executions, that data set is probably not statistically similar.

2. If measurements from a test are noticeably higher or lower, when charted side-by-side, than the results of the other test executions, it is probably not statistically similar.

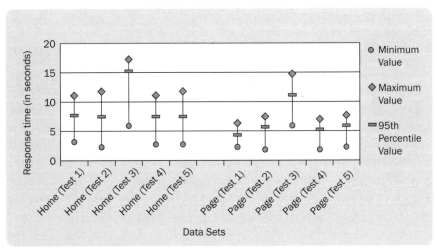

Figure 15.7 *Result Comparison*

3. If one data set for a particular item (e.g., the response time for a single page) in a test is noticeably higher or lower, but the results for the data sets of the remaining items appear similar, the test itself is probably statistically similar (even though it is probably worth the time to investigate the reasons for the difference of the one dissimilar data set.

Statistical Equivalence

The method above for determining statistical significance actually is applying the principle of statistical equivalence. Essentially, the process outlined above for determining statistical significance could be restated as "Given results data from multiple tests intended to be equivalent, the data from any one of those tests may be treated as statistically significant if that data is statistically equivalent to 80 percent or more of all the tests intended to be equivalent." Mathematical determination of equivalence using such formal methods as chi-squared and t-tests are not common on commercial software development projects. Rather, it is generally deemed acceptable to estimate equivalence by using charts similar to those used to determine statistical significance.

Statistical Outliers

From a purely statistical point of view, any measurement that falls outside of three standard deviations, or 99 percent, of all collected measurements is considered an *outlier*. The problem with this definition is that it assumes that the collected measurements are both statistically significant and distributed normally, which is not at all automatic when evaluating performance test data.

For the purposes of this explanation, a more applicable definition of an outlier from a StatSoft, Inc. (*http://www.statsoftinc.com*) is the following:
Outliers are atypical, infrequent observations: data points which do not appear to follow the distribution of the rest of the sample. These may represent consistent but rare traits, or be the result of measurement errors or other anomalies which should not be modeled.

Note that this (or any other) description of outliers only applies to data that is deemed to be a statistically significant sample of measurements. Without a statistically significant sample, there is no generally acceptable approach to determining the difference between an outlier and a representative measurement.

Using this description, results graphs can be used to determine evidence of outliers—occasional data points that just don't seem to belong. A reasonable approach to determining if any apparent outliers are truly atypical and infrequent is to re-execute the tests and then compare the results to the first set. If the majority of the measurements are the same, except for the potential outliers, the results are likely to contain genuine outliers that can be disregarded. However, if the results show similar potential outliers, these are probably valid measurements that deserve consideration.

After identifying that a dataset appears to contain outliers, the next question is, how many outliers can be dismissed as "atypical infrequent observations?"

There is no set number of outliers that can be unilaterally dismissed, but rather a maximum percentage of the total number of observations. Applying the spirit of the two definitions above, a reasonable conclusion would be that up to 1 percent of the total values for a particular measurement that are outside of three standard deviations from the mean are significantly atypical and infrequent enough to be considered outliers.

In summary, in practice for commercially driven software development, it is generally acceptable to say that values representing less than 1 percent of all the measurements for a particular item that are at least three standard deviations off the mean are candidates for omission in results analysis if (and only if) identical values are not found in previous or subsequent tests. To express the same concept in a more colloquial way: obviously rare and strange data points that can't immediately be explained, account for a very small part of the results, and are not identical to any results from other tests are probably outliers.

A note of caution: identifying a data point as an outlier and excluding it from results summaries does not imply ignoring the data point. Excluded outliers should be tracked in some manner appropriate to the project context in order to determine, as more tests are conducted, if a pattern of concern is identified in what by all indications are outliers for individual tests.

Confidence Intervals

Because determining levels of confidence in data is even more complex and time-consuming than determining statistical significance or the existence of outliers, it is extremely rare to make such a determination during commercial software projects. A confidence interval for a specific statistic is the range of values around the statistic where the 'true' statistic is likely to be located within a given level of certainty.

Because stakeholders do frequently ask for some indication of the presumed accuracy of test results—for example, what is the confidence interval for these results?—another commonsense approach must be employed.

When performance testing, the answer to that question is directly related to the accuracy of the model tested. Since in many cases the accuracy of the model cannot be reasonably determined until after the software is released into production, this is not a particularly useful dependency. However, there is a way to demonstrate a confidence interval in the results.

By testing a variety of scenarios, including what the team determines to be "best," "worst," and "expected" cases in terms of the measurements being collected, a graphical depiction of a confidence interval can be created, similar to the one below.

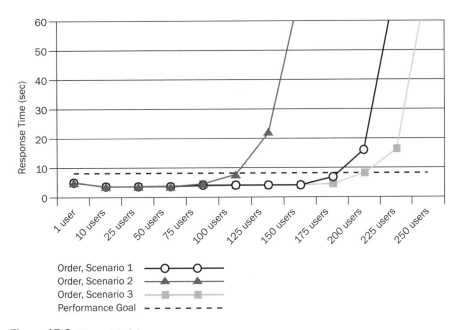

Figure 15.8 *Usage Models*

In this graph, a dashed line represents the performance goal, and the three curves represent the results from the worst-case (most performance-intensive), best-case (least performance-intensive), and expected-case user community models. As one would expect, the blue curve from the expected case falls between the best- and worst-case curves. Observing where these curves cross the red line, one can see how many users can access the system in each case while still meeting the stated performance goal. If the team is 95-percent confident (by their own estimation) that the best- and worst-case user community models are truly best- and worst-case, this chart can be read as follows: the tests show, with 95-percent confidence, that between 100 and 200 users can access the system while experiencing acceptable performance.

Although a confidence interval of between 100 and 200 users might seem quite large, it is important to note that without empirical data representing the actual production usage, it is unreasonable to expect higher confidence in results than there is in the models that generate those results. The best that one can do is to be 100-percent confident that the test results accurately represent the model being tested.

Summary

Members of software development teams, developers, testers, administrators, and managers alike need to know how to apply mathematics and interpret statistical data in order to do their jobs effectively. Performance analysis and reporting are particularly math-intensive. It is critical that mathematical and statistical concepts in performance testing be understood so that correct performance-testing analysis and reporting can be done.

16

Performance Test Reporting Fundamentals

Objectives

- Learn how to apply principles of effective reporting to performance test data.
- Learn when to share technical results versus produce stakeholder reports.
- Learn what questions various team members expect performance reports to answer.

Overview

Managers and stakeholders need more than simply the results from various tests—they need conclusions based on those results, and consolidated data that supports those conclusions. Technical team members also need more than just results—they need analysis, comparisons, and details of how the results were obtained. Team members of all types get value from performance results being shared more frequently. In this chapter, you will learn how to satisfy the needs of all the consumers of performance test results and data by employing a variety of reporting and results-sharing techniques, and by learning exemplar scenarios where each technique tends be well received.

How to Use This Chapter

Use this chapter to understand the principles of effective performance test results reporting, and as a reference for exemplars of effective data presentation. To get the most from this chapter:

- Use the "Principles of Effective Reporting" section to understand the key concepts and principles behind effective reporting.
- Use the "Frequently Reported Performance Data" section to learn about various ways that performance data can be presented and the types of results to which those methods are most effectively applied.
- Use the "Questions to Be Answered by Reporting" section to understand how reports are designed for various audiences, and how to deliver the right information to the right audience in a format that they find intuitive.

Principles of Effective Reporting

The key to effective reporting is to present information of interest to the intended audience in a quick, simple, and intuitive manner. The following are some of underlying principles of effective reporting:

- Report early, report often
- Report visually
- Report intuitively
- Use the right statistics
- Consolidate data correctly
- Summarize data effectively
- Customize reports for the intended audience
- Use concise verbal summaries
- Make the data available

Report Early, Report Often

Continual sharing of information and data is critical to the efficiency and overall success of a performance-testing project. However, not all of the information and data to be shared needs to take the form of a formal or semiformal report. One effective approach is to send stakeholders summary charts and tables every day or two in an e-mail message that contains a concise statement of key points. Use the feedback and questions you receive from those stakeholders when deciding what to put in the next formal or semiformal report. In this way you can gauge the needs of your audience before writing what is intended to be a stand-alone or final document.

Sharing information and data with the technical team can be an even more straightforward process. It may be as simple as posting the location of the new results files to a team wiki before you begin analyzing them, and then posting links to any charts and graphs that derive from your analysis.

Report Visually

Most people find that data and statistics reported in a graphical format are easier to digest. This is especially true of performance results data, where the volume of data is frequently very large and most significant findings result from detecting patterns in the data. It is possible to find these patterns by scanning through tables or by using complex mathematical algorithms, but the human eye is far quicker and more accurate in the vast majority of cases.

Once a pattern or "point of interest" has been identified visually, you will typically want to isolate that pattern by removing the remaining "chart noise." In this context, chart noise includes all of the data points representing activities and time slices that contain no points of interest (that is, the ones that look like you expect them to). Removing the chart noise enables you to more clearly evaluate the pattern you are interested in, and makes reports more clear.

Report Intuitively

Whether formal or informal, reports should be able to stand on their own. If a report leaves the reader with questions as to why the information is important, the report has failed. While reports do not need to provide the answers to issues to be effective, the issues should be quickly and intuitively clear from the presentation.

One method to validate the intuitiveness of a report is to remove all labels or identifiers from charts and graphs and all identifying information from narratives and then present the report to someone unfamiliar with the project. If that person is able to quickly and correctly point to the issue of concern in the chart or graph, or identify why the issue discussed in the narrative is relevant, then you have created an intuitive report.

Use the Right Statistics

Even though there is a widespread need to understand many statistical concepts, many software developers, testers, and managers either do not have strong backgrounds in or do not enjoy statistics. This can lead to significant misrepresentations of performance test results when reporting. If you are not sure what statistics to use to highlight a particular issue, do not hesitate to ask for assistance.

Consolidate Data Correctly

While it is not strictly necessary to consolidate results, it tends to be much easier to demonstrate patterns in results when those results are consolidated into one or two graphs rather than distributed over dozens. That said, it is important to remember that only results from identical test executions that are statistically similar can be consolidated into performance report output tables and charts.

Additional Considerations

In order for results to be consolidated, both the test and the test environment must be identical, and the test results must be statistically equivalent. One approach to determining if results are similar enough to be consolidated is to compare results from at least five test executions and apply the following rules:

- If more than 20 percent (or one out of five) of the test execution results appear *not* to be similar to the rest, something is generally wrong with the test environment, the application, or the test itself.
- If a 95th percentile value for any test execution is greater than the maximum or less than the minimum value for any of the other test executions, it is not statistically similar.
- If every page/timer result in a test execution is noticeably higher or lower on the chart than the results of all the rest of the test executions, it is not statistically similar.
- If a single page/timer result in a test execution is noticeably higher or lower on the chart than all the rest of the test execution results, but the results for all the rest of the pages/timers in that test execution are not, the test executions are probably statistically similar.

Summarize Data Effectively

Summarizing results frequently makes it much easier to demonstrate meaningful patterns in the test results. Summary charts and tables present data from different test executions side by side so that trends and patterns are easy to identify. The overall point of these tables and charts is to show team members how the test results compare to the performance goals of the system so they can make important decisions about taking the system live, upgrading the system, or even, in some cases, completely reevaluating the project.

Additional Considerations

Keep the following key points in mind when summarizing test data:

- Use charts and tables that make your findings clear.
- Use text to supplement tables and charts, not the other way around.
- If a chart or table is confusing to the reader, don't use it.

Customize Reports for the Intended Audience

Performance test results are most commonly read by one of three audiences: technical team members, non-technical team members, and stakeholders outside of the core team. These three groups tend to look for very different things in a performance report and are inclined to prefer different presentation methods. When reporting, make sure that you identify which group or groups you are reporting to and what their expectations are before deciding on the best way to present the results you have collected.

Use Concise Verbal Summaries

Results should have at least a short verbal summary associated with them, and some results are best or most easily presented in writing alone. What you decide to include in that text depends entirely on your intended audience. Some audiences may require just one or two sentences capturing the key point(s) you are trying to make with the graphic. For example:

"From observing this graph, you can see that the system under test meets all stated performance goals up to 150 hourly users but at that point degrades quickly to an essentially unusable state."

Other audiences may also require a detailed explanation of the graph being presented. For example:

"In this graph, you see the average response time in seconds, portrayed vertically on the left side of the graph, plotted against the total number of hourly users simulated during each test execution, portrayed horizontally along the bottom of the graph. The intersection points depict..."

Make the Data Available

There is a disturbingly popular belief that performance testing (or other testing) data should not be shared in its raw form out of fear that the consumers of that data will use or analyze it improperly. While this concern is not invalid, of much greater concern is the fact that it is simply not reasonable to expect any one person or team to be able to extract all of the value from a set of data at one point in time. Data provides different value to different people at different times, and the only way to get the most out of the data is to make that data continually available to the team. Additionally, making the data available tends to minimize some people's perception that the performance results are simply fabrications based on a set of tools and processes that they do not understand.

Frequently Reported Performance Data

The following are the most frequently reported types of results data. The sections that follow describe what makes this data interesting to whom, as well as considerations for reporting that type of data.

- End-user response times
- Resource utilizations
- Volumes, capacities, and rates
- Component response times
- Trends

End-user Response Times

End-user response time is by far the most commonly requested and reported metric in performance testing. If you have captured goals and requirements effectively, this is a measure of presumed user satisfaction with the performance characteristics of the system or application. Stakeholders are interested in end-user response times to judge the degree to which users will be satisfied with the application. Technical team members are interested because they want to know if they are achieving the overall performance goals from a user's perspective, and if not, in what areas those goals not being met.

Exemplar1

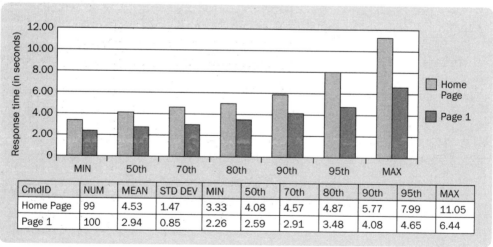

CmdID	NUM	MEAN	STD DEV	MIN	50th	70th	80th	90th	95th	MAX
Home Page	99	4.53	1.47	3.33	4.08	4.57	4.87	5.77	7.99	11.05
Page 1	100	2.94	0.85	2.26	2.59	2.91	3.48	4.08	4.65	6.44

Figure 16.1 *Response Time*

Exemplar2

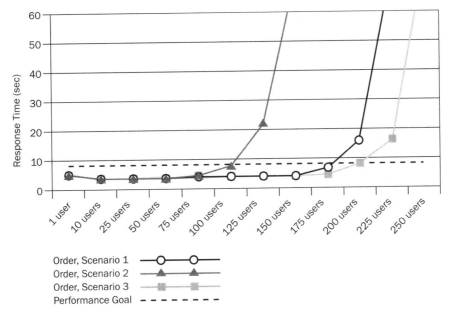

Figure 16.2 *Response Time Degradation*

Considerations

Even though end-user response times are the most commonly reported performance-testing metric, there are still important points to consider.

- **Eliminate outliers before reporting.** Even one legitimate outlier can dramatically skew your results.

- **Ensure that the statistics are clearly communicated.** The difference between an average and a 90th percentile, for example, can easily be the difference between "ship it" and "fix it."

- **Report abandonment separately.** If you are accounting for user abandonment, the collected response times for abandoned pages may not represent the same activity as non-abandoned pages. To be safe, report response times for non-abandoned pages with an end-user response time graph and response times and abandonment percentages by page on a separate graph or table.

- **Report every page or transaction separately.** Even though some pages may appear to represent an equivalence class, there could be differences that you are unaware of.

Resource Utilizations

Resource utilizations are the second most requested and reported metrics in performance testing. Most frequently, resource utilization metrics are reported verbally or in a narrative fashion. For example, "The CPU utilization of the application server never exceeded 45 percent. The target is to stay below 70 percent." It is generally valuable to report resource utilizations graphically when there is an issue to be communicated.

Exemplar for Stakeholders

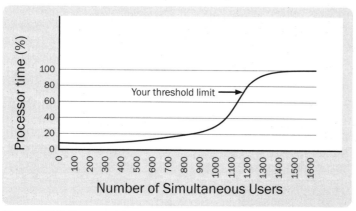

Figure 16.3 *Processor Time*

Exemplar for Technical Team Members

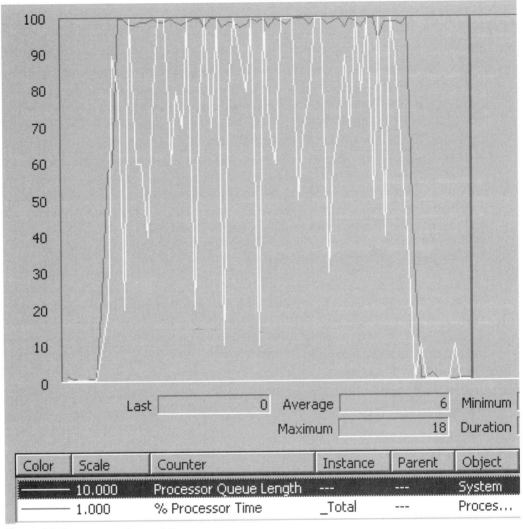

Figure 16.4 *Processor Time and Queue*

Additional Considerations

Points to consider when reporting resource utilizations include:

- **Know when to report all of the data and when to summarize.** Very often, simply reporting the peak value for a monitored resource during the course of a test is adequate. Unless an issue is detected, the report only needs to demonstrate that the correct metrics were collected to detect the issue if it were present during the test.

- **Overlay resource utilization metrics with other load and response data.** Resource utilization metrics are most powerful when presented on the same graph as load and/or response time data. If there is a performance issue, this helps to identify relationships across various metrics.

- **If you decide to present more than one data point, present them all.** Resource utilization rates will often change dramatically from one measurement to the next. The pattern of change across measurements is at least as important as the current value. Moving averages and trend lines obfuscate these patterns, which can lead to incorrect assumptions and regrettable decisions.

Volumes, Capacities, and Rates

Volume, capacity, and rate metrics are also frequently requested by stakeholders, even though the implications of these metrics are often more challenging to interpret. For this reason, it is important to report these metrics in relation to specific performance criteria or a specific performance issue. Some examples of commonly requested volume, capacity, and rate metrics include:

- Bandwidth consumed
- Throughput
- Transactions per second
- Hits per second
- Number of supported registered users
- Number of records/items able to be stored in the database

Exemplar

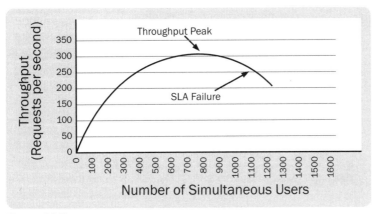

Figure 16.5 *Throughput*

Additional Considerations

Points to consider when reporting volumes, capacities and rates include:

- **Report metrics in context.** Volume, capacity, and rate metrics typically have little stand-alone value.
- **Have test conditions and supporting data available.** While this is a good idea in general, it is particularly important with volume, capacity, and rate metrics.
- **Include narrative summaries with implications.** Again, while this is a good idea in general, it is virtually critical to ensure understanding of volume, capacity, and rate metrics.

Component Response Times

Even though component response times are not reported to stakeholders as commonly as end-user response times or resource utilization metrics, they are frequently collected and shared with the technical team. These response times help developers, architects, database administrators (DBAs), and administrators determine what sub-part or parts of the system are responsible for the majority of end-user response times.

Exemplar

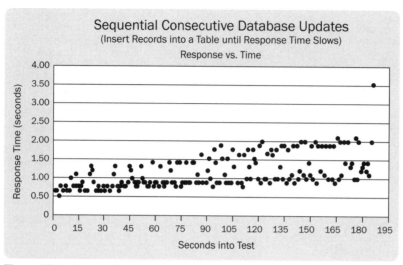

Figure 16.6 *Sequential Consecutive Database Updates*

Additional Considerations

Points to consider when reporting component response times include:

- **Relate component response times to end-user activities.** Because it is not always obvious what end-user activities are impacted by a component's response time, it is a good idea to include those relationships in your report.

- **Explain the degree to which the component response time matters.** Sometimes the concern is that a component might become a bottleneck under load because it is processing too slowly; at other times, the concern is that end-user response times are noticeably degraded as a result of the component. Knowing which of these conditions applies to your project enables you to make effective decisions.

Trends

Trends are one of the most powerful but least-frequently used data-reporting methods. Trends can show whether performance is improving or degrading from build to build, or the rate of degradation as load increases. Trends can help technical team members quickly understand whether the changes they recently made achieved the desired performance impact.

Exemplar

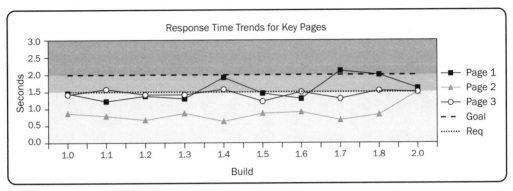

Figure 16.7 *Response Time Trends for Key Pages*

Additional Considerations

Points to consider when reporting trends include:

- **Trends typically do not add value until there are at least three measurements.** Sometimes trends cannot be effectively detected until there are more than three measurements. Start creating your trend charts with the first set of data, but be cautious about including them in formal reports until you have collected enough data for there to be an actual trend to report.

- **Share trends with the technical team before including them in formal reports.** This is another generally good practice, but it is particularly relevant to trends because developers, architects, administrators, and DBAs often will have already backed out a change that caused the trend to move in the wrong direction before they are able to compile their report. In this case, you can decide that the trend report is not worth including, or you can simply make an annotation describing the cause and stating that the issue has already been resolved.

Questions to Be Answered By Reporting

Almost every team member has unique wants, needs, and expectations when it comes to reporting data and results obtained through performance testing. While this makes sharing information obtained through performance testing challenging, knowing what various team members expect and value in advance makes providing valuable information to the right people, at the right level of detail and at the right time, much easier

All Roles

Some questions that are commonly posed by team members include:

- *Is performance getting better or worse?*
- *Have we met the requirements/service level agreements (SLAs)?*
- *What reports are available?*
- *How frequently can I get reports?*
- *Can I get a report with more/less detail?*

Executive Stakeholders

Executive stakeholders tend to have very specific reporting needs and expectations that are often quite different from those of other team members. Stakeholders tend to prefer information in small, digestible chunks that clearly highlight the key points. Additionally, stakeholders like visual representations of data that are intuitive at a glance, as well as "sound bite"–size explanations of those visual representations. Finally, stakeholders tend to prefer consolidated and summarized information on a less frequent (though not significantly less frequent) basis than other team members. The following are common questions that executive stakeholders want performance test reports to answer:

- *Is this ready to ship?*
- *How will these results relate to production?*
- *How much confidence should I have in these results?*
- *What needs to be done to get this ready to ship?*
- *Is the performance testing proceeding as anticipated?*
- *Is the performance testing adding value?*

Project-Level Managers

Project-level managers—including the project manager, development lead or manager, and the test lead or manager—have all of the same needs and questions as the executive stakeholders, except that they want the answers more frequently and in more detail. Additionally, they commonly want to know the following:

- *Are performance issues being detected efficiently?*
- *Are performance issues being resolved efficiently?*
- *What performance testing should we be conducting that we currently are not?*
- *What performance testing are we currently doing that is not adding value?*
- *Are there currently any blockers? If so, what are they?*

Technical Team Members

Although technical team members have some degree of interest in all of the questions posed by managers and stakeholders, they are more interested in receiving a continual flow of information related to test results, monitored data, observations, and opportunities for analysis and improvement. Technical team members tend to want to know the following:

- *What do these results mean to my specialty/focus area?*
- *Where can I go to see the results for the last test?*
- *Where can I go to get the raw data?*
- *Can you capture metric X during the next test run?*

Types of Results Sharing

In the most basic sense, there are three distinct types of results sharing: raw data display, technical reports, and stakeholder reports. While all are based on timely, accurate, and relevant communication of results, observations, concerns, and recommendations, each type targets a different audience, and the most effective methods of communicating data differ dramatically.

Raw Data Display

While not explicitly a reporting scenario, the sharing of raw data for collaboration purposes involves many of the same principles of data presentation that are applied to reports in order to improve the effectiveness of the collaboration.

In general, most people would rather view data and statistics in graphical form instead of in tables. In some cases, however, tables are the most efficient way to show calculated results for all of the data. It is recommended that you use tables sparingly in reports, while including the tabular form of the data used to create charts and graphs as an appendix or attachment to a report, so that interested stakeholders can refer to it.

Results from the following types of tests can be well represented in a tabular format:

- Baseline
- Benchmark
- Scalability
- Any other user-experience–based test

Tables are an excellent way to present volumes of data in a clean and orderly manner and to support the findings they ultimately lead to. However, you should be careful not to overuse tables in your reports. Many people quickly skip over tables and read only the surrounding text or examine only the charts that go with them. Be certain that whether you use the tables discussed below or other types, you present in your report only those tables that clearly make an important point. Huge tables containing all of the supporting data may be of interest to a few individuals, but not to most, and thus should be included only in an appendix to a report. Raw data is most commonly shared in the following formats:

- Spreadsheets
- Text files (and regular expression searches)
- Data collection tools ("canned" reports)

Technical Reports

Technical reports are generally more formal than raw data display, but not excessively so. Technical reports should stand on their own, but since they are intended for technical members of the team who are currently working on the project, they do not need to contain all of the supplemental detail that a stakeholder report normally does. In the simplest sense, technical reports are made up of the following:

- Description of the test, including workload model and test environment
- Easily digestible data with minimal pre-processing
- Access to the complete data set and test conditions
- Short statements of observations, concerns, questions, and requests for collaboration

Technical reports most commonly include data in the following formats:

- Scatter plots
- Pareto charts
- Trend charts
- Summary spreadsheets

Stakeholder Reports

Stakeholder reports are the most formal of the performance data sharing formats. These reports must be able to stand alone while at the same time being intuitive to someone who is not working on the project in a day-to-day technical role. Typically, these reports center on acceptance criteria and risks. To be effective, stakeholder reports typically need to include:

- The acceptance criteria to which the results relate
- Intuitive, visual representations of the most relevant data
- A brief verbal summary of the chart or graph in terms of criteria

- Intuitive, visual representations of the workload model and test environment
- Access to associated technical reports, complete data sets, and test conditions
- A summary of observations, concerns, and recommendations

When preparing stakeholder reports, consider that most stakeholder reports meet with one (or more) of the following three reactions. All three are positive in their own way but may not seem to be at first. These reactions and some recommended responses follow:

- **"These are great, but where's the supporting data?"** This is the most common response from a technical stakeholder. Many people and organizations want to have all of the data so that they can draw their own conclusions. Fortunately, this is an easy question to handle: simply include the entire spreadsheet with this supporting data as an appendix to the report.

- **"Very pretty, but what do they mean?"** This is where text explanations are useful. People who are not familiar with performance testing or performance results often need to have the implications of the results spelled out for them. Remember that more than 90 percent of the times, performance testers are the bearers of bad news that the stakeholder was not expecting. The tester has the responsibility to ensure that the stakeholder has confidence in the findings, as well as presenting this news in a constructive manner.

- **"Terrific! This is exactly what I wanted! Don't worry about the final report—these will do nicely."** While this *seems* like a blessing, do not take it as one. Sooner or later, your tables and charts will be presented to someone who asks one of the two preceding questions, or worse, asks how the data was obtained. If there is not at least a final report that tells people where to find the rest of the data, people will question the results because you are not present to answer those questions.

Creating a Technical Report

Although six key components of a technical report are listed below, all six may not be appropriate for every technical report. Similarly, there may be additional information that should be included based on exactly what message you are trying to convey with the report. While these six components will result in successful technical reports most of the time, remember that sometimes creativity is needed to make your message clear and intuitive.

Consider including the following key components when preparing a technical report:

- A results graph
- A table for single-instance measurements (e.g., maximum throughput achieved)
- Workload model (graphic)

- Test environment (annotated graphic)
- Short statements of observations, concerns, questions, and requests for collaboration
- References section

Exemplar Results Graph

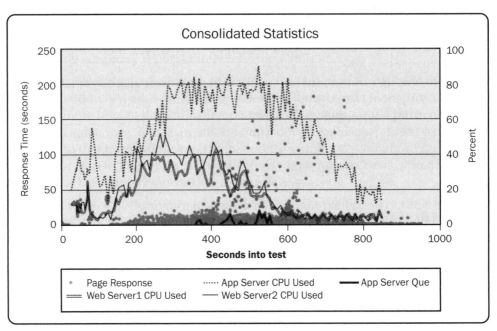

Figure 16.8 *Consolidated Statistics*

Exemplar Tables for Single-Instance Measurements

Additional Metrics	
Maximum Running Vusers:	125
Total Throughput (bytes):	179,746,398
Average Throughput (bytes/second):	322,126
Total Hits:	26,500
Average hits per second:	47.491

Figure 16.9 *Single Instance Measurements*

Exemplar Workload Model Graphic

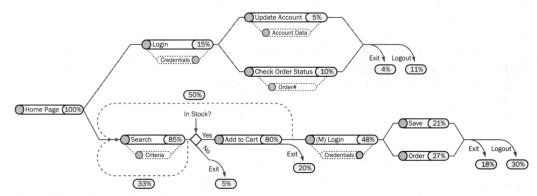

Figure 16.10 *Workload Model*

Exemplar Test Environment Graphic

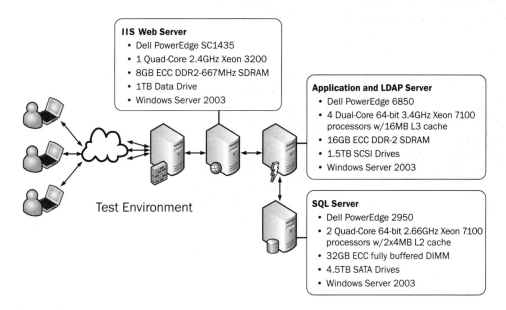

Figure 16.11 *Test Environment*

Exemplar Summary Statement

"The results graph shows both response times and resource utilization together. Close examination shows that Application Server CPU Usage and queue length coincide with significantly degraded response time. It appears as if the application server CPU usage was the catalyst to the degradation, but this has yet to be confirmed. The remaining charts and graphs are included as supplemental information for easy reference."

Exemplar References Section

"Raw data and additional supporting information is checked into the version-control system with the build and tagged as PerfTest-{date}-{issue number}."

Creating a Stakeholder Report

Although eight key components of a stakeholder report are listed below, all eight may not be appropriate for every stakeholder report. Similarly, there may be additional information that should be included based on exactly what message you are trying to convey with the report. While these eight components will result in successful stakeholder reports most of the time, remember that sometimes creativity is needed to make your message clear and intuitive.

Consider including the following key components when preparing a stakeholder report:

- Criteria to which the results relate
- A results graph
- A table for single-instance measurements (e.g., maximum throughput achieved)
- A brief verbal summary of the chart or graph in terms of criteria
- Workload model (graphic)
- Test environment (annotated graphic)
- Summary of observations, concerns, and recommendations
- References section

Exemplar Criteria Statement

"This report relates to end-user response time compliances as documented in the requirements management system as requirements Perf### through Perf??? at one-half of the expected peak load with the most commonly expected usage scenario."

Exemplar Results Graph

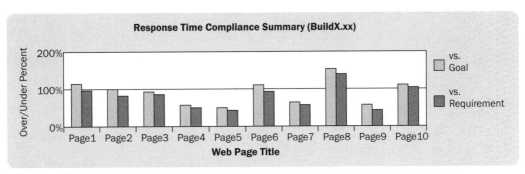

Figure 16.12 *Response Time Compliance Summary*

Exemplar Tables for Single-Instance Measurements

Supporting Metrics	Max. Vusers		125
	Peak	**Average**	**Target**
CPU Utilization: Web Server1	42%	18%	<75%
CPU Utilization: Web Server2	53%	21%	<75%
CPU Utilization: Application Server	89%	48%	<75%
Queue: Application Server	23	2	1

Figure 16.13 *Single Instance Measurements*

Exemplar Criteria-Based Results Summary

"All metrics collected achieved their required values except for the response times of pages 8 and 10.

- *Page 10 failed to achieve its required value by 2 percent.*
- *Page 8 failed to achieve its required value by 38 percent."*

Exemplar Workload Model Graphic

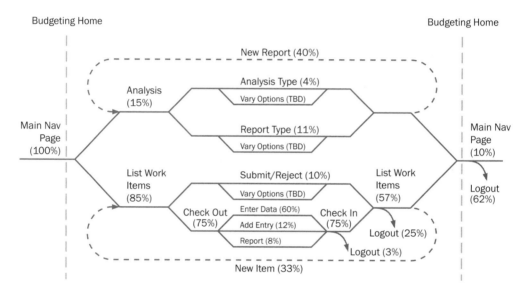

Figure 16.14 *Workload Model*

Exemplar Test Environment Graphic

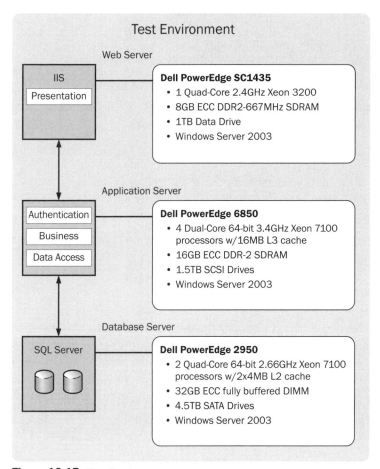

Figure 16.15 *Test Environment*

Exemplar Observations and Recommendations Statement

"Based on the test conditions and results, the performance testing and tuning team recommends the following.

1. *Continue performance testing with increasingly strenuous scenarios and loads.*

2. *Priority should be given to determining the root cause of pages 8 and 10 not achieving their acceptance criteria, and subsequently tuning those root causes.*

3. *At such time as additional pages demonstrate a failure to achieve their acceptance criteria, a dedicated root cause and tuning cycle should be undertaken."*

Exemplar References Section

"All of the data used to create this report and execute the tests that generated that data is checked into the version-control system as read-only with the release candidate and tagged as PerfTest-{date}-{RC number}-Validation.

"The same data has been temporarily copied to {\\shared-resource\location} for individuals without access to the version-control system."

Summary

Performance test reporting is the process of presenting results data that will support key technological and business decisions. The key to creating effective reports is to consider the audience of the data before determining how best to present the data. The most effective performance-test results will present analysis, comparisons, and details behind how the results were obtained, and will influence critical business decision-making.

Part VIII

Performance Testing Techniques

In this part:

- Load Testing Web Applications
- Stress Testing Web Applications

17

Load-Testing Web Applications

Objectives

- Understand the key concepts of load testing.
- Learn how to load-test a Web application.

Overview

This chapter explains how to load-test a Web application. Load testing helps to identify the maximum operating capacity of an application as well as any bottlenecks that might interfere with its operating at capacity. The basic approach to performing load testing on a Web application is:

1. Identify the performance-critical scenarios.
2. Identify the workload profile for distributing the entire load among the key scenarios.
3. Identify the metrics that you want to collect in order to verify them against your performance objectives.
4. Design tests to simulate the load.
5. Use tools to implement the load according to the designed tests, and capture the metrics.
6. Analyze the metric data captured during the tests.

By using an iterative testing process, these steps should help you achieve your performance objectives.

There are many reasons for load-testing a Web application. The most basic type of load testing is used to determine the Web application's behavior under both normal and anticipated peak load conditions. As you begin load testing, it is recommended that you start with a small number of virtual users and then incrementally increase the load from normal to peak. You can then observe how your application performs during this gradually increasing load condition. Eventually, you will cross a threshold limit for your performance objectives. For example, you might continue to increase the load until the server processor utilization reaches 75 percent, or when end-user response times exceed 8 seconds.

How to Use This Chapter

Use this chapter to understand the key concepts of load testing and the steps involved in load-testing Web applications. To get the most from this chapter:

- Use the "Input" and "Output" sections to understand the key inputs for load testing a Web application and the key outcomes of doing so.
- Use the "Approach for Load Testing" section to get an overview of the approach for load testing a Web application, and as quick reference guide for you and your team.
- Use the various steps sections to understand the details of each step involved in load-testing a Web application.

Input

The following are useful inputs for load-testing a Web application:

- Performance-critical usage scenarios
- Workload models
- Performance acceptance criteria
- Performance metrics associated with the acceptance criteria
- Interview feedback from the designer or developer of the Web application
- Interview feedback from end users of the application
- Interview feedback from the operations personnel who will maintain and manage the application

Output

The main outcomes that load testing helps you to accomplish are:

- Updated test plans and test designs for load and performance testing
- Various performance measures such as throughput, response time, and resource utilization

- Potential bottlenecks that need to be analyzed in the white-box testing phase
- The behavior of the application at various load levels

Approach for Load Testing

The following steps are involved in load-testing a Web application:

1. Step 1—Identify performance acceptance criteria
2. Step 2—Identify key scenarios
3. Step 3—Create a workload model
4. Step 4—Identify the target load levels
5. Step 5—Identify metrics
6. Step 6—Design specific tests
7. Step 7—Run tests
8. Step 8—Analyze the results

These steps are graphically represented below. The sections that follow discuss each step in detail.

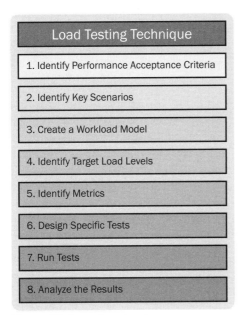

Figure 17.1 *Load Testing Steps*

Step 1—Identify Performance Acceptance Criteria

Identifying performance acceptance criteria is most valuable when initiated early in the application's development life cycle. It is frequently valuable to record the acceptance criteria for your application and store them in a place and format that is available to the entire team for review and comment. Criteria are typically determined by balancing your business, industry, technology, competitive, and user requirements.

Test objectives frequently include the following:

- **Response time.** For example, the product catalog must be displayed in less than 3 seconds.
- **Throughput.** For example, the system must support 100 transactions per second.
- **Resource utilization.** A frequently overlooked aspect is the amount of resources your application is consuming, in terms of processor, memory, disk input output (I/O), and network I/O.
- **Maximum user load.** This test objective determines how many users can run on a specific hardware configuration.
- **Business related metrics.** This objective is mapped to business volume at normal and peak values; for example, the number of orders or Help desk calls handled at a given time.

Step 2—Identify Key Scenarios

Scenarios are anticipated user paths that generally incorporate multiple application activities. Key scenarios are those for which you have specific performance goals, those considered to be high-risk, those that are most commonly used, or those with a significant performance impact. The basic steps for identifying key scenarios are.

1. Identify all the scenarios for a Web application. For example, even the most basic e-commerce application must support the following user scenarios:
   - Browse catalog
   - Search for a product
   - Place an order
2. Identify the activities involved in each of the scenarios. For example, a "Place an Order" scenario will include the following activities:
   - Log on to the application.
   - Browse the product catalog.
   - Search for a specific product.
   - Add items to the shopping cart.
   - Validate credit card details and place an order.

3. Identify the scenarios that are most commonly executed or most resource-intensive; these will be the key scenarios used for load testing. For example, in an e-commerce application, browsing a catalog may be the most commonly executed scenario, whereas placing an order may be the most resource-intensive scenario because it accesses the database.

- The most commonly executed scenarios for an existing Web application can be determined by examining the log files.

- The most commonly executed scenarios for a new Web application can be obtained from market research, historical data, market trends, and so on.

- Resource-intensive scenarios can be identified by using design documents or the actual code implementation. The primary resources are:

  - Processor
  - Memory
  - Disk I/O
  - Network I/O

Once they have been identified, you will use these key scenarios to create workload profiles and to design load tests.

Step 3—Create a Workload Model

When defining workload distribution, consider the following key points for determining the characteristics for user scenarios:

- A user scenario is defined as a navigational path, including intermediate steps or activities, taken by the user to complete a task. This can also be thought of as a user session.

- A user will typically pause between pages during a session. This is known as *user delay* or *think time*.

- A session will have an average duration when viewed across multiple users. It is important to account for this when defining the load levels that will translate into concurrent usage, overlapping users, or user sessions per unit of time.

- Not all scenarios can be performed by a new user, a returning user, or either; know who you expect your primary users to be and test accordingly.

Step 4—Identify Target Load Levels

Identify the load levels to be applied to the workload distribution(s) identified during the previous step. The purpose of identifying target load levels is to ensure that your tests can be used to predict or compare a variety of production load conditions. The following are common inputs used for determining target load levels:

- Business volume (both current and projected) as it relates to your performance objectives
- Key scenarios
- Distribution of work
- Session characteristics (navigational path, duration, percentage of new users)

By combining the items above, you can determine the remaining details necessary to implement the workload model under a particular target load.

Step 5—Identify Metrics

There is a virtually unlimited number of metrics that can be collected during a performance test execution. However, collecting too many metrics can make analysis unwieldy as well as negatively impact the application's actual performance. For these reasons, it is important to identify the metrics that are most relevant to your performance objectives and those that you anticipate will help you to identify bottlenecks. Only well-selected metrics that are analyzed correctly and contextually provide information of value.

The following are a few suggestions for identifying the metrics that will provide the most valuable information to your project:

- **Define questions related to your application performance that can be easily tested.** For example, what is the checkout response time when placing an order? How many orders are placed in a minute? These questions have definite answers.
- **With the answers to these questions, determine quality goals for comparison against external expectations.** For example, checkout response time should be 30 seconds, and a maximum of 10 orders should be placed in a minute. The answers are based on market research, historical data, market trends, and so on.
- **Identify the metrics.** Using your list of performance-related questions and answers, identify the metrics that provide information related to those questions and answers.

- **Identify supporting metrics.** Using the same approach, you can identify lower-level metrics that focus on measuring the performance and identifying the bottlenecks in the system. When identifying low-level metrics, most teams find it valuable to determine a baseline for those metrics under single-user and/or normal load conditions. This helps you determine the acceptable load levels for your application. Baseline values help you analyze your application performance at varying load levels and serve as a starting point for trend analysis across builds or releases.

- **Reevaluate the metrics to be collected regularly.** Goals, priorities, risks, and current issues are bound to change over the course of a project. With each of these changes, different metrics may provide more value than the ones that have previously been identified.

Additionally, to evaluate the performance of your application in more detail and to identify potential bottlenecks, it is frequently useful to monitor metrics in the following categories:

- **Network-specific metrics.** This set of metrics provides information about the overall health and efficiency of your network, including routers, switches, and gateways.

- **System-related metrics.** This set of metrics helps you identify the resource utilization on your server. The resources being utilized are processor, memory, disk I/O, and network I/O.

- **Platform-specific metrics.** Platform-specific metrics are related to software that is used to host your application, such as the Microsoft .NET Framework common language runtime (CLR) and ASP.NET-related metrics.

- **Application-specific metrics.** These include custom performance counters inserted in your application code to monitor application health and identify performance issues. You might use custom counters to determine the number of concurrent threads waiting to acquire a particular lock, or the number of requests queued to make an outbound call to a Web service.

- **Service-level metrics.** These metrics can help to measure overall application throughput and latency, or they might be tied to specific business scenarios.

- **Business metrics.** These metrics are indicators of business-related information, such as the number of orders placed in a given timeframe.

Step 6—Design Specific Tests

Using your scenarios, key metrics, and workload analysis, you can now design "specific tests to be conducted. Each test will generally have a different purpose, collect different data, include different scenarios, and have different target load levels. The key is to design tests that will help the team collect the information it needs in order to understand, evaluate, or tune the application.

Points to consider when designing tests include:

- Do not change your test design because the design is difficult to implement in your tool.

- If you cannot implement your test as designed, ensure that you record the details pertaining to the test that you do implement.

- Ensure that the model contains all of the supplementary data needed to create the actual test.

- Consider including invalid data in your performance tests. For example, include some users who mistype their password on the first attempt but get it correct on a second try.

- First-time users usually spend significantly more time on each page or activity than experienced users.

- The best possible test data is test data collected from a production database or log file.

- Think about nonhuman system users and batch processes as well as end users. For example, there might be a batch process that runs to update the status of orders while users are performing activities on the site. In this situation, you would need to account for those processes because they might be consuming resources.

- Do not get overly caught up in striving for perfection, and do not fall into the trap of oversimplification. In general, it is a good idea to start executing tests when you have a reasonable test designed and then enhance the design incrementally while collecting results.

Step 7—Run Tests

Poor load simulations can render all of the work in the previous activities useless. To understand the data collected from a test execution, the load simulation must reflect the test design. When the simulation does not reflect the test design, the results are prone to misinterpretation. Consider the following steps when preparing to simulate load:

1. Configure the test environment in such a way that it mirrors your production environment as closely as possible, noting and accounting for all differences between the two.

2. Ensure that performance counters relevant for identified metrics and resource utilization are being measured and are not interfering with the accuracy of the simulation.

3. Use appropriate load-generation tools to create a load with the characteristics specified in your test design.

4. Using the load-generation tool(s), execute tests by first building up to the target load specified in your test design, in order to validate the correctness of the simulation. Some things to consider during test execution include:

   • Begin load testing with a small number of users distributed against your user profile, and then incrementally increase the load. It is important to allow time for the system to stabilize between increases in load while evaluating the correctness of the simulation.

   • Consider continuing to increase the load and record the behavior until you reach the threshold for the resources identified in your performance objectives, even if that load is beyond the target load specified in the test design. Information about when the system crosses identified thresholds is just as important as the value of the metrics at the target load of the test.

   • Similarly, it is frequently valuable to continue to increase the number of users until you run up against the service-level limits beyond which you would be violating your SLAs for throughput, response time, and resource utilization.

Note: Make sure that the client computers (agents) you use to generate load are not overly stressed. Resource utilization such as processor and memory must remain well below the utilization threshold values to ensure accurate test results.

Step 8—Analyze the Results

You can analyze the test results to find performance bottlenecks between each test run or after all testing has been completed. Analyzing the results correctly requires training and experience with graphing correlated response time and system data.

The following are the steps for analyzing the data:

1. Analyze the captured data and compare the results against the metric's accepted level to determine whether the performance of the application being tested shows a trend toward or away from the performance objectives.

2. Analyze the measured metrics to diagnose potential bottlenecks. Based on the analysis, if required, capture additional metrics in subsequent test cycles. For example, suppose that during the first iteration of load tests, the process shows a marked increase in memory consumption, indicating a possible memory leak. In the subsequent iterations, additional memory counters related to generations can be captured to study the memory allocation pattern for the application.

Summary

Load testing helps to identify the maximum operating capacity of the application and any bottlenecks that might be degrading performance.

The basic methodology for performing load testing on a Web application is to identify the performance-critical key scenarios; identify the workload profile for distributing all the load among the key scenarios; identify metrics that you want to collect in order to verify them against your performance objectives; create test cases that will be used to simulate the load test; use tools to simulate the load according to the test cases and capture the metrics; and finally, analyze the metrics data captured during the tests.

18

Stress Testing Web Applications

Objectives

- Understand the key concepts of stress testing.
- Learn how to stress-test a Web application.

Overview

Stress testing is a type of performance testing focused on determining an application's robustness, availability, and reliability under extreme conditions. The goal of stress testing is to identify application issues that arise or become apparent only under extreme conditions. These conditions can include heavy loads, high concurrency, or limited computational resources. Proper stress testing is useful in finding synchronization and timing bugs, interlock problems, priority problems, and resource loss bugs. The idea is to stress a system to the breaking point in order to find bugs that will make that break potentially harmful. The system is not expected to process the overload without adequate resources, but to behave (e.g., fail) in an acceptable manner (e.g., not corrupting or losing data).

Stress tests typically involve simulating one or more key production scenarios under a variety of stressful conditions. For example, you might deploy your application on a server that is already running a processor-intensive application; in this way, your application is immediately "starved" of processor resources and must compete with the other application for processor cycles. You can also stress-test a single Web page or even a single item such as a stored procedure or class.

This chapter presents a high-level introduction to stress-testing a Web application. Stress testing can help you identify application issues that surface only under extreme conditions.

Examples of Stress Conditions

Examples of stress conditions include:

- Excessive volume in terms of either users or data; examples might include a denial of service (DoS) attack or a situation where a widely viewed news item prompts a large number of users to visit a Web site during a three-minute period.
- Resource reduction such as a disk drive failure.
- Unexpected sequencing.
- Unexpected outages/outage recovery.

Examples of Stress-Related Symptoms

Examples of stress-related symptoms include:

- Data is lost or corrupted.
- Resource utilization remains unacceptably high after the stress is removed.
- Application components fail to respond.
- Unhandled exceptions are presented to the end user.

How to Use This Chapter

Use this chapter to understand the key concepts of stress testing and the steps involved in stress-testing a Web application. To get the most from this chapter:

- Use the "Input" and "Output" sections to understand the key inputs for stress-testing a Web application and the key outcomes of this type of testing.
- Use the "Approach for Stress Testing" section to get an overview of the approach for stress-testing a Web application, and as quick reference guide for you and your team.
- Use the various steps sections to understand the details of each step involved in stress-testing a Web application.
- Use the "Usage Scenario for Stress Testing" section to understand various real-world scenarios where stress testing is employed.

Input

To perform stress testing, you are likely to use as reference one or more of the following items:

- Results from previous stress tests
- Application usage characteristics (scenarios)
- Concerns about those scenarios under extreme conditions

- Workload profile characteristics
- Current peak load capacity (obtained from load testing)
- Hardware and network architecture and data
- Disaster-risk assessment (e.g., likelihood of blackouts, earthquakes, etc.)

Output

Output from a stress test may include:

- Measures of the application under stressful conditions
- Symptoms of the application under stress
- Information the team can use to address robustness, availability, and reliability

Approach for Stress Testing

The following steps are involved in stress-testing a Web application:

1. **Step 1 - Identify test objectives.** Identify the objectives of stress testing in terms of the desired outcomes of the testing activity.

2. **Step 2 - Identify key scenario(s).** Identify the application scenario or cases that need to be stress-tested to identify potential problems.

3. **Step 3 - Identify the workload.** Identify the workload that you want to apply to the scenarios identified during the "Identify objectives" step. This is based on the workload and peak load capacity inputs.

4. **Step 4 - Identify metrics.** Identify the metrics that you want to collect about the application's performance. Base these metrics on the potential problems identified for the scenarios you identified during the "Identify objectives" step.

5. **Step 5 - Create test cases.** Create the test cases in which you define steps for running a single test, as well as your expected results.

6. **Step 6 - Simulate load.** Use test tools to simulate the required load for each test case and capture the metric data results.

7. **Step 7 - Analyze results.** Analyze the metric data captured during the test.

These steps are graphically represented below; the following sections discuss each step in detail.

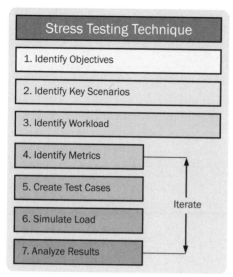

Figure 18.1 *Stress Testing Steps*

Step 1—Identify Test Objectives

Asking yourself or others the following questions can help in identifying the desired outcomes of your stress testing:

1. *Is the purpose of the test to identify the ways the system can possibly fail catastrophically in production?*

2. *Is it to provide information to the team in order to build defenses against catastrophic failures?*

3. *Is it to identify how the application behaves when system resources such as memory, disk space, network bandwidth, or processor cycles are depleted?*

4. *Is it to ensure that functionality does not break under stress?* For example, there may be cases where operational performance metrics meet the objectives, but the functionality of the application is failing to meet them—orders are not inserted in the database, the application is not returning the complete product information in searches, form controls are not being populated properly, redirects to custom error pages are occurring during the stress testing, and so on.

Step 2—Identify Key Scenario(s)

To get the most value out of a stress test, the test needs to focus on the behavior of the usage scenario or scenarios that matter most to the overall success of the application. To identify these scenarios, you generally start by defining a single scenario that you want to stress-test in order to identify a potential performance issue. Consider these guidelines when choosing appropriate scenarios:

- Select scenarios based on how critical they are to overall application performance.
- Try to test those operations that are most likely to affect performance. These might include operations that perform intensive locking and synchronization, long transactions, and disk-intensive input/output (I/O) operations.
- Base your scenario selection on the specific areas of your application identified as potential bottlenecks by load-testing data. Although you should have fine-tuned and removed the bottlenecks after load testing, you should still stress-test the system in these areas to verify how well your changes handle extreme stress levels.

Examples of scenarios that may need to be stress tested separately from other usage scenarios for a typical e-commerce application include the following:

- An order-processing scenario that updates the inventory for a particular product. This functionality has the potential to exhibit locking and synchronization problems.
- A scenario that pages through search results based on user queries. If a user specifies a particularly wide query, there could be a large impact on memory utilization. For example, memory utilization could be affected if a query returns an entire data table.

Step 3—Identify the Workload

The load you apply to a particular scenario should stress the system sufficiently beyond threshold limits to enable you to observe the consequences of the stress condition. One method to determine the load at which an application begins to exhibit signs of stress is to incrementally increase the load and observe the application behavior under various load conditions. The key is to systematically test with various workloads until you create a significant failure. These variations may be accomplished by adding more users, reducing delay times, adding or reducing the number and type of user activities represented, or adjusting test data.

For example, a stress test could be designed to simulate every registered user of the application attempting to log on during one 30-second period. This would simulate a situation where the application suddenly became available again after a period of downtime and all users were anxiously refreshing their browsers, waiting for the application to come back online. Although this situation does not occur frequently in the real world, it does happen often enough for there to be real value in learning how the application will respond if it does.

Remember to represent the workload with accurate and realistic test data—type and volume, different user logins, product IDs, product categories, and so on—allowing you to simulate important failures such as deadlocks or resource consumption.

The following activities are generally useful in identifying appropriate workloads for stress testing:

- **Identify the distribution of work.** For each key scenario, identify the distribution of work to be simulated. The distribution is based on the number and type of users executing the scenario during the stress test.

- **Estimate peak user loads.** Identify the maximum expected number of users during peak load conditions for the application. Using the work distribution you identified for each scenario, calculate the percentage of user load per key scenario.

- **Identify the anti-profile.** As an alternative, you can start by applying an anti-profile to the normal workload. In an *anti-profile*, the workload distributions are inverted for the scenario under consideration. For example, if the normal load for the order-processing scenario is 10 percent of the total workload, the anti-profile would be 90 percent of the total workload. The remaining load can be distributed among the other scenarios. Using an anti-profile can serve as a valuable starting point for your stress tests because it ensures that the critical scenarios are subjected to loads beyond the normal load conditions.

Step 4—Identify Metrics

When identified and captured correctly, metrics provide information about how well or poorly your application is performing as compared to your performance objectives. In addition, metrics can help you identify problem areas and bottlenecks within your application.

Using the desired performance characteristics identified during the "Identify objectives" step, identify metrics to be captured that focus on potential pitfalls for each scenario. The metrics can be related to both performance and throughput goals as well as providing information about potential problems; for example, custom performance counters that have been embedded in the application.

When identifying metrics, you will use either direct objectives or indicators that are directly or indirectly related to those objectives. The following table describes performance metrics in terms of related performance objectives.

Performance metrics	Category
Base set of metrics	
Processor	• Processor utilization
Process	• Memory consumption • Processor utilization • Process recycles
Memory	• Memory available • Memory utilization
Disk	• Disk utilization
Network	• Network utilization
Transactions/business metrics	• Transactions/sec • Transactions succeeded • Transactions failed • Orders succeeded • Orders failed
Threading	• Contentions per second • Deadlocks • Thread allocation
Response times	• Transactions times

Step 5—Create Test Cases

Identifying workload profiles and key scenarios generally does not provide all of the information necessary to implement and execute test cases. Additional inputs for completely designing a stress test include performance objectives, workload characteristics, test data, test environments, and identified metrics. Each test design should mention the expected results and/or the key data of interest to be collected, in such a way that each test case can be marked as a "pass," "fail," or "inconclusive" after execution.

The following is an example of a test case based on the order-placement scenario.

Test 1—Place Order Scenario

Workload: 1,000 simultaneous users.

Think time: Use a random think time between 1 and 10 seconds in the test script after each operation.

Test Duration: Run the test for two days.

Expected results:

- Application hosting process should not recycle because of deadlock or memory consumption.
- Throughput should not fall below 35 requests per second.

- Response time should not be greater than 7 seconds for 95 percent of total transactions completed.

- "Server busy" errors should not be more than 10 percent of the total response because of contention-related issues.

- Order transactions should not fail during test execution. Database entries should match the "Transactions succeeded" count.

Step 6—Simulate Load

After you have completed the previous steps to an appropriate degree, you should be ready to simulate the load executing the stress test. Typically, test execution follows these steps:

1. Validate that the test environment matches the configuration that you were expecting and/or designed your test for.

2. Ensure that both the test and the test environment are correctly configured for metrics collection.

3. Before running the test, execute a quick "smoke test" to make sure that the test script and remote performance counters are working correctly.

4. Reset the system (unless your scenario is to do otherwise) and start a formal test execution.

Note: Make sure that the client (a.k.a. load generator) computers that you use to generate load are not overly stressed. Utilization of resources such as processor and memory should remain low enough to ensure that the load-generation environment is not itself a bottleneck.

Step 7—Analyze Results

Analyze the captured data and compare the results against the metric's accepted level. If the results indicate that your required performance levels have not been attained, analyze and fix the cause of the bottleneck. To address observed issues, you might need to do one or more of the following:

- Perform a design review.

- Perform a code review.

- Run stress tests in environments where it is possible to debug possible causes of failures, during test execution.

In situations where performance issues are observed, but only under conditions that are deemed to be unlikely enough to warrant tuning at the current time, you may want to consider conducting additional tests to identify an early indicator for the issue in order to avoid unwanted surprises.

Usage Scenarios for Stress Testing

The following are examples of how stress testing is applied in practice:

- **Application stress testing.** This type of test typically focuses on more than one transaction on the system under stress, without the isolation of components. With application stress testing, you are likely to uncover defects related to data locking and blocking, network congestion, and performance bottlenecks on different components or methods across the entire application. Because the test scope is a single application, it is common to use this type of stress testing after a robust application load-testing effort, or as a last test phase for capacity planning. It is also common to find defects related to race conditions and general memory leaks from shared code or components.

- **Transactional stress testing.** Transactional stress tests aim at working at a transactional level with load volumes that go beyond those of the anticipated production operations. These tests are focused on validating behavior under stressful conditions, such as high load with same resource constraints, when testing the entire application. Because the test isolates an individual transaction, or group of transactions, it allows for a very specific understanding of throughput capacities and other characteristics for individual components without the added complication of inter-component interactions that occurs in testing at the application level. These tests are useful for tuning, optimizing, and finding error conditions at the specific component level.

- **Systemic stress testing.** In this type of test, stress or extreme load conditions are generated across multiple applications running on the same system, thereby pushing the boundaries of the applications' expected capabilities to an extreme. The goal of systemic stress testing is to uncover defects in situations where different applications block one another and compete for system resources such as memory, processor cycles, disk space, and network bandwidth. This type of testing is also known as *integration stress testing* or *consolidation stress testing*. In large-scale systemic stress tests, you stress all of the applications together in the same consolidated environment. Some organizations choose to perform this type of testing in a larger test lab facility, sometimes with the hardware or software vendor's assistance.

Exploratory Stress Testing

Exploratory stress testing is an approach to subjecting a system, application, or component to a set of unusual parameters or conditions that are unlikely to occur in the real world but are nevertheless possible. In general, exploratory testing can be viewed as an interactive process of simultaneous learning, test design, and test execution. Most often, exploratory stress tests are designed by modifying existing tests and/or working with application/system administrators to create unlikely but possible conditions in the system. This type of stress testing is seldom conducted in isolation because it is typically conducted to determine if more systematic stress testing is called for related to a particular failure mode. The following are some examples of exploratory stress tests to determine the answer to "How will the system respond if...?"

- All of the users logged on at the same time.
- The load balancer suddenly failed.
- All of the servers started their scheduled virus scan at the same time during a period of peak load.
- The database went offline during peak usage.

Summary

Stress testing allows you to identify potential application issues that surface only under extreme conditions. Such conditions range from exhaustion of system resources such as memory, processor cycles, network bandwidth, and disk capacity to excessive load due to unpredictable usage patterns, common in Web applications.

Stress testing centers around objectives and key user scenarios with an emphasis on the robustness, reliability, and stability of the application. The effectiveness of stress testing relies on applying the correct methodology and being able to effectively analyze testing results. Applying the correct methodology is dependent on the capacity for reproducing workload conditions for both user load and volume of data, reproducing key scenarios, and interpreting the key performance metrics.

Index

risks, 24
see also Web application load-testing
load-testing Web applications *see* Web application load-testing

M

Mariani, Rico, xvii-xviii
mathematical principles, 199-210
  arithmetic means, 202-203
  averages, 202-203
  bell curves, 205
  confidence intervals, 209-210
  data sets, 200-203
  linear distributions, 204-205
  means, 202-203
  medians, 203
  normal distributions, 205
  normal values, 204
  outliers, 207-208
  percentiles, 203
  reliability, 206-207
  result comparison, 207
  standard deviations, 204
  statistical equivalence, 207
  statistical outliers, 207-208
  statistical significance, 206-207
  uniform distributions, 204-205
  usage models, 209
means, 202-203
medians, 203
metrics, 14
  see also application usage modeling; end-user response time goals
modeling *see* application usage modeling

N

normal distributions, 205
normal values, 204

O

objectives, 117-129
  architecture review, 120-121

capturing or estimating resource budgets, 122-123
capturing or estimating resource usage targets and thresholds, 121-122
case studies, 124-128
  2 million user visits per hour, 127-128
  Enterprise Resource Planning (ERP) software upgrade, 125
  multiple branch offices, 126-127
communicating results, 124
identifying metrics, 123
project plan review, 120
staying aware of changing objectives, targets, and budgets, 124
terminology, 118-119
order-placement scenario, 253-254
organization, xxii-xxiii
outliers, 207-208

P

percentiles, 203
performance, 14, 142-143
performance acceptance criteria *see* acceptance criteria
performance budgets, 119
performance objectives described, 118
performance requirements, 14
performance targets, 119, 143
performance testing, 3-4, 10
  benefits, 20
  categories of, 10-11
  core activities, 4-6
  defined, 18
  key types of, 18-20
  objectives, 14, 118, 143
  overview, 3
  purpose, 6-7, 18
  summary table of activities, 35
  tuning, 9-10
  types of, 17-22

see also CMMI; iterative performance activities; risks; Web application testing
performance thresholds, 14, 119, 143
processor time and queue, 219
project context, 7-8
project vision, 69-70
project-level managers, 224
purpose, xx

R

reliability described, 206-207
reporting, 211-234
  component response times, 221-222
  concise verbal summaries, 215
  customizing for the intended audience, 215
  data availability, 215
  data consolidation, 214
  effectiveness, 212-215
  exemplar observations and recommendations statement, 232
  exemplar references section, 231-234
  frequently reported data, 216-223
    component response times, 221-222
    end-user response times, 216-217
    processor time and queue, 219
    resource utilizations, 218-220
    response time chart, 216
    response time degradation, 217
    trends, 222-223
    volumes, capacities, and rates, 220-221
  intuitiveness, 213
  questions to be answered by reporting, 223-225
    all roles, 224
    executive stakeholders, 224